FAZAL SHEIKH

FAZAL SHEIKH

ETHER

STEIDL

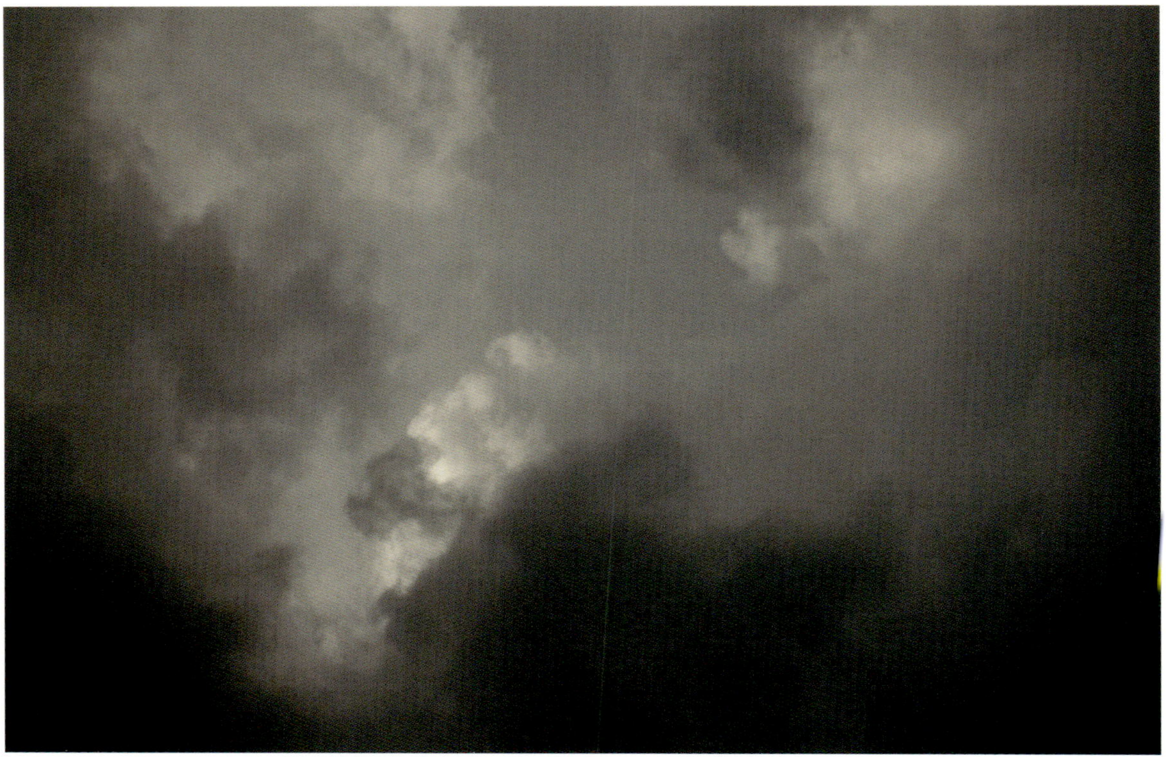

Night-walking in Benares 2008 – 2012

✷

Sheikh Fazal Ilahi
July 22 1897 – March 22 1955

Karam Bibi Sheikh
1903 – April 8 1985

Winthrop Carver Lenz
June 9 1906 – February 1 1994

Lila Fowler Southard Lenz
March 8 1912 – July 16 1991

Abdul Majied Sheikh
August 3 1940 – August 6 2003

Henrietta Southard Lenz Sheikh
November 22 1940 – July 12 1987

✷

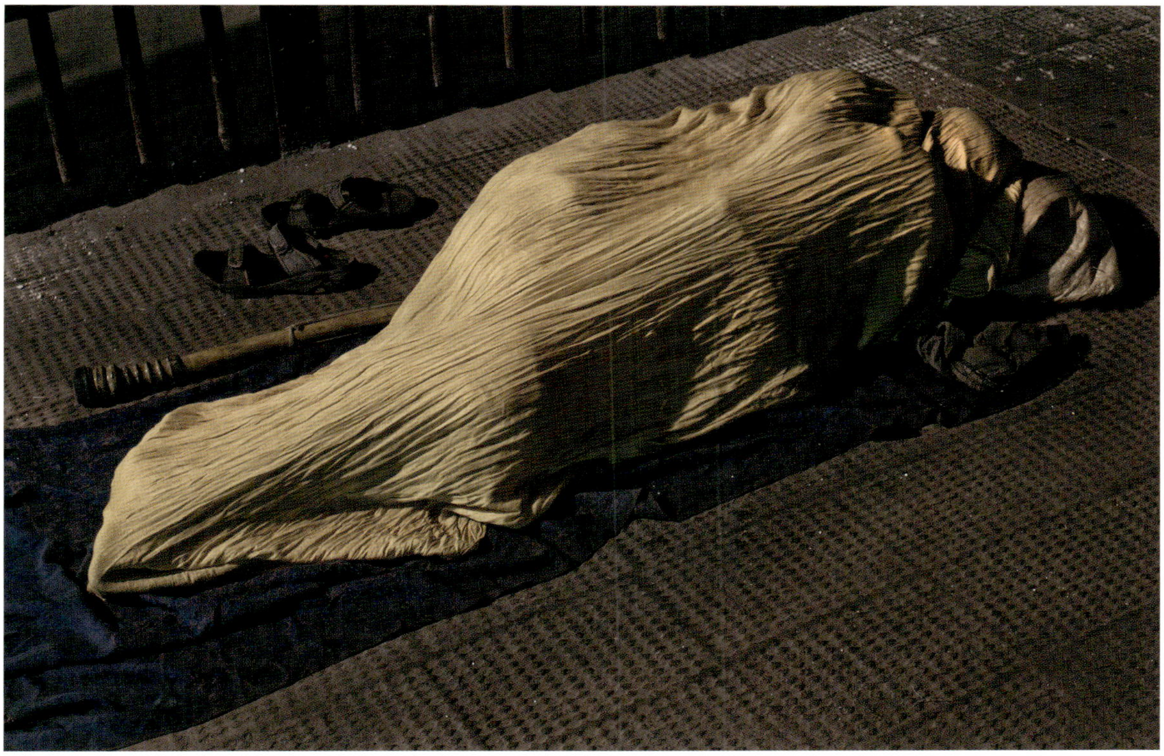

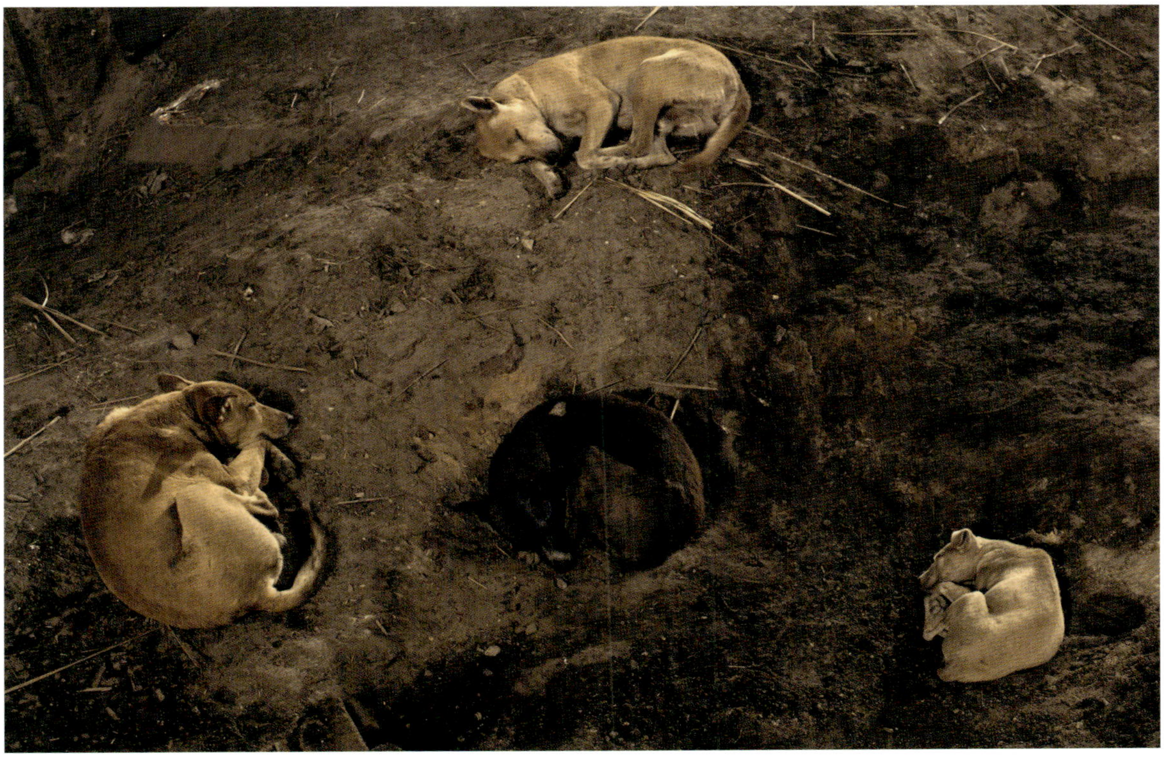

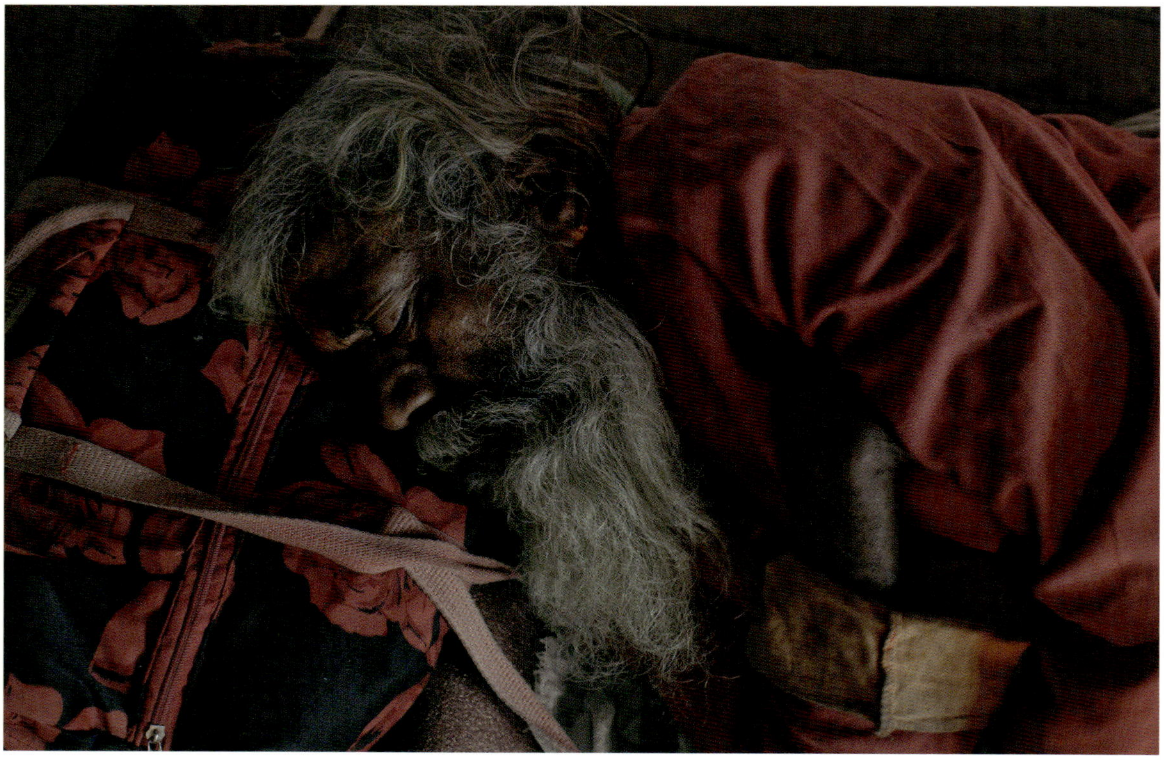

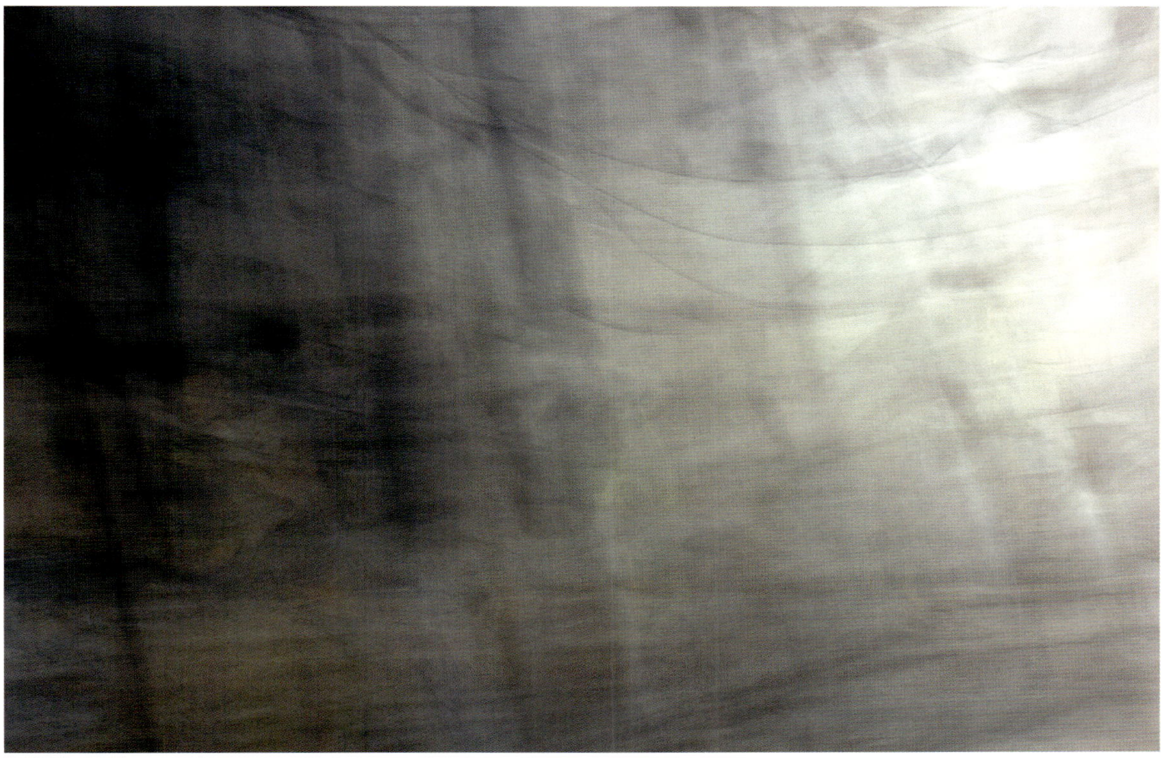

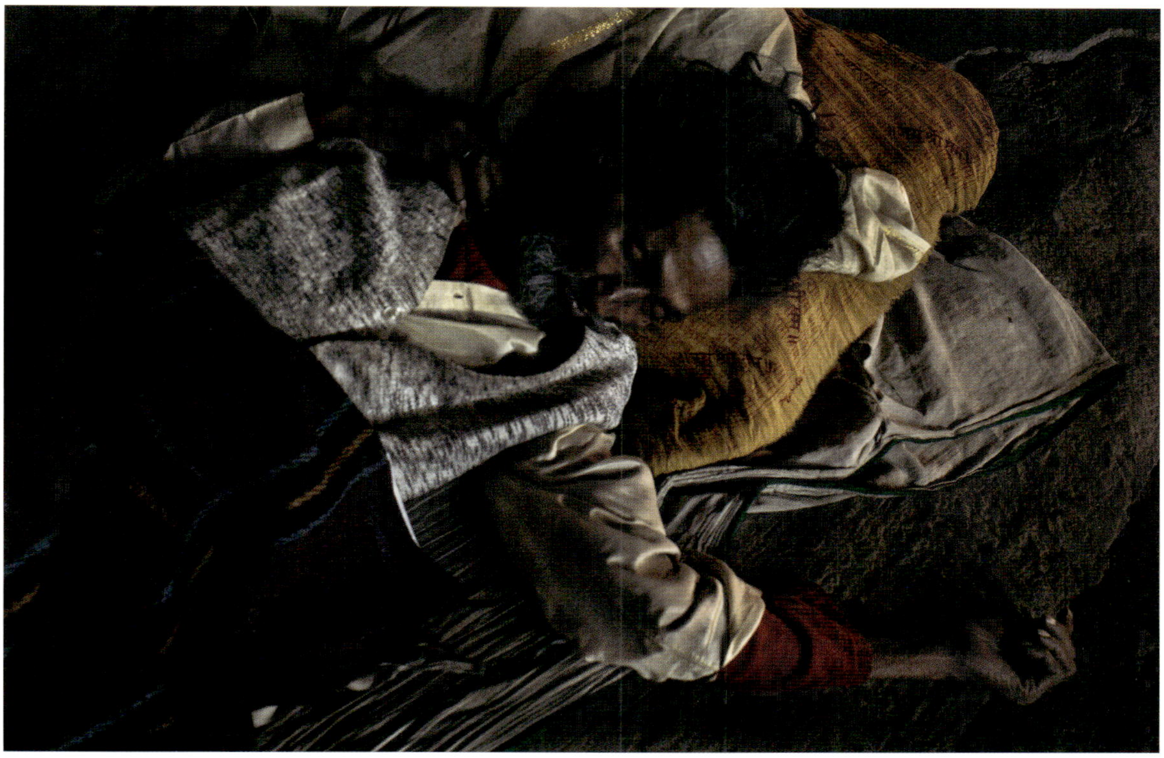

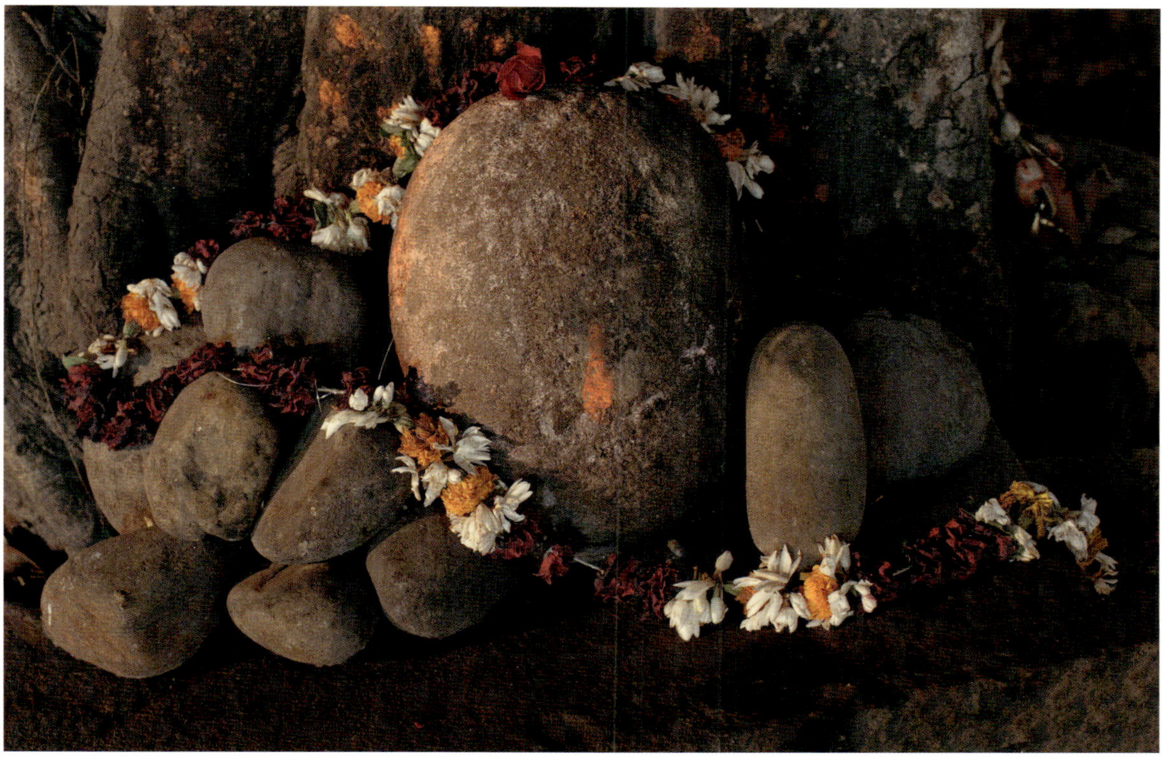

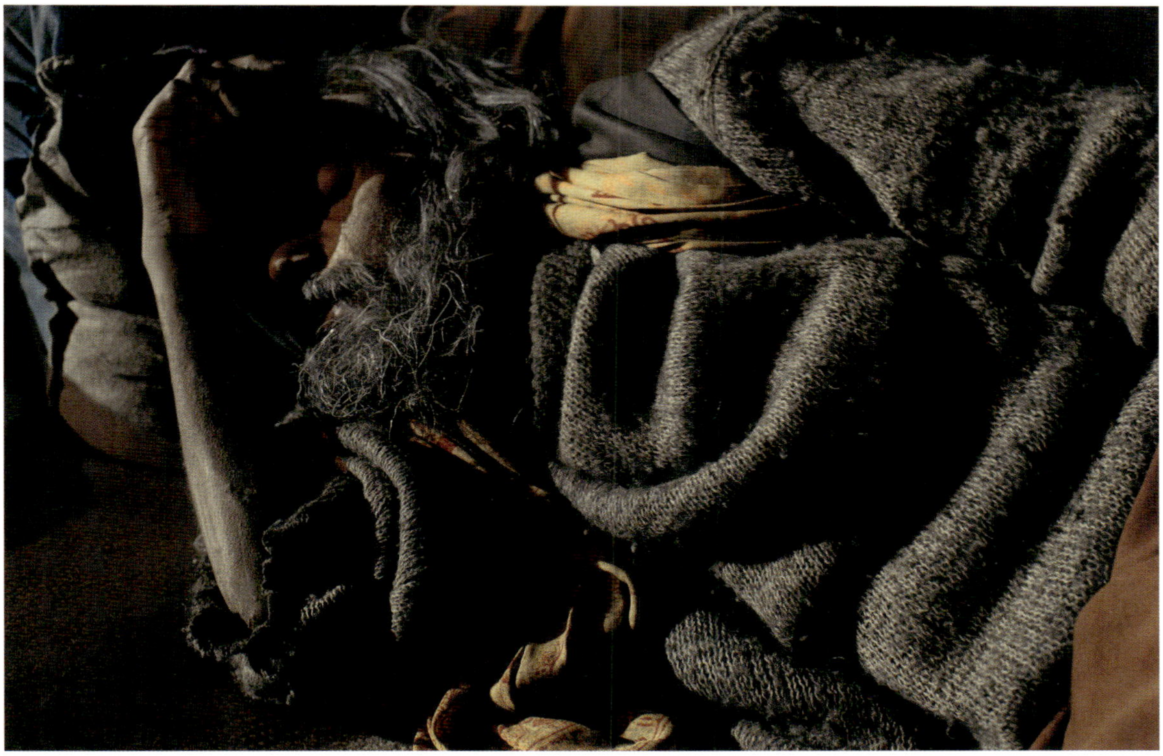

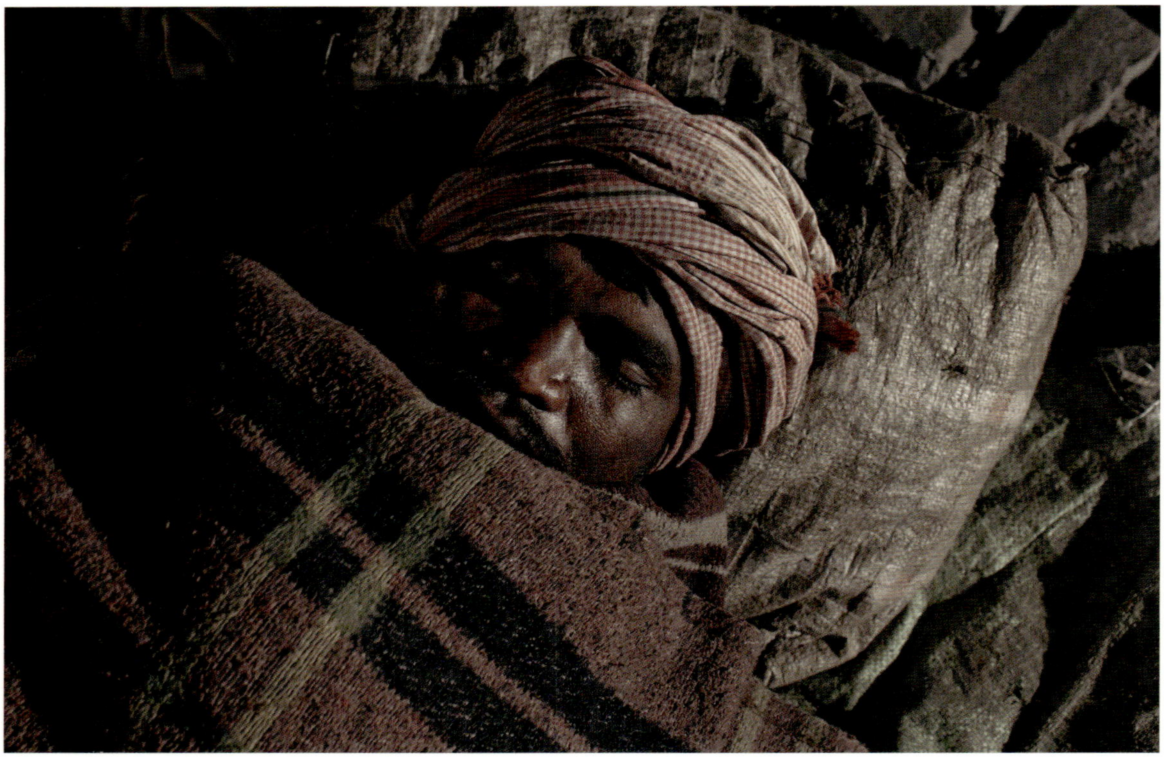

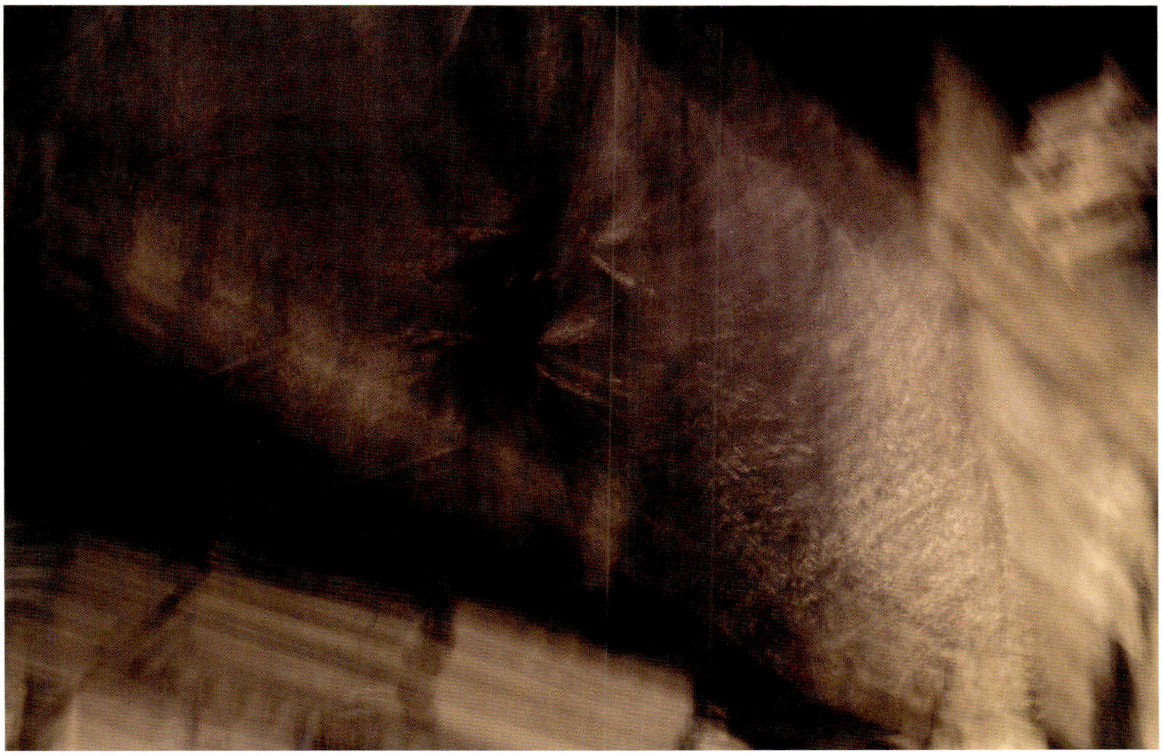

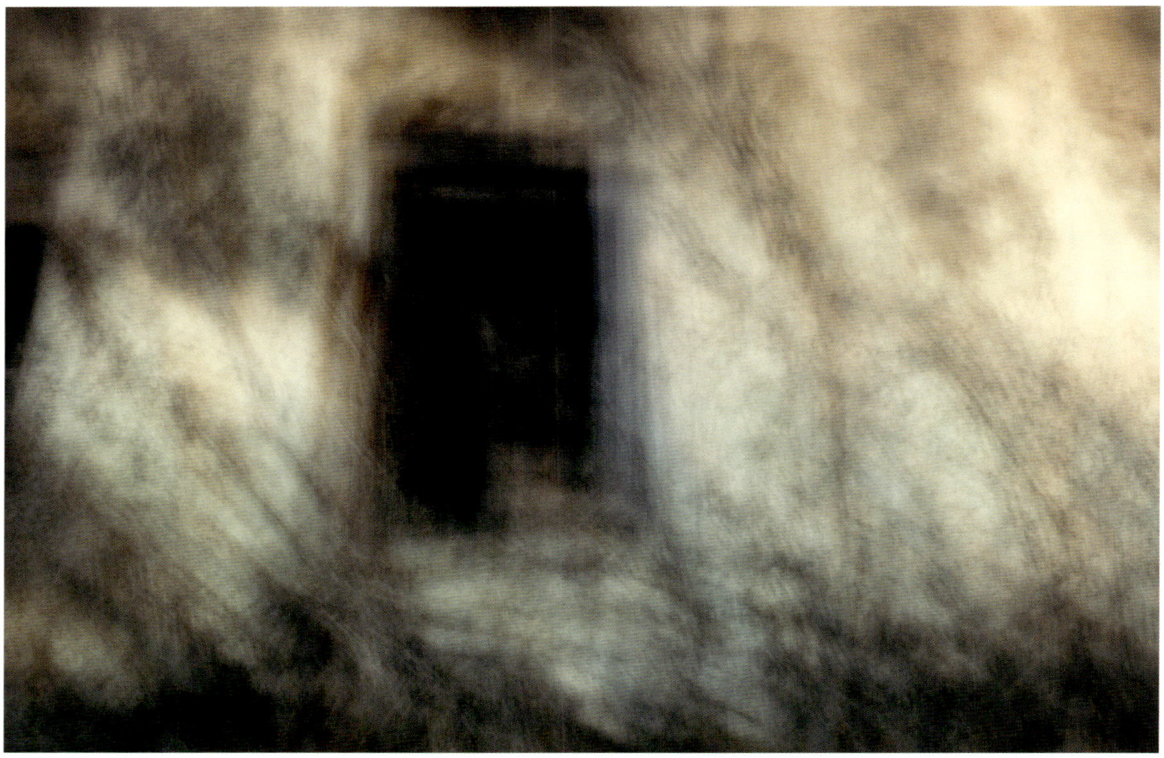

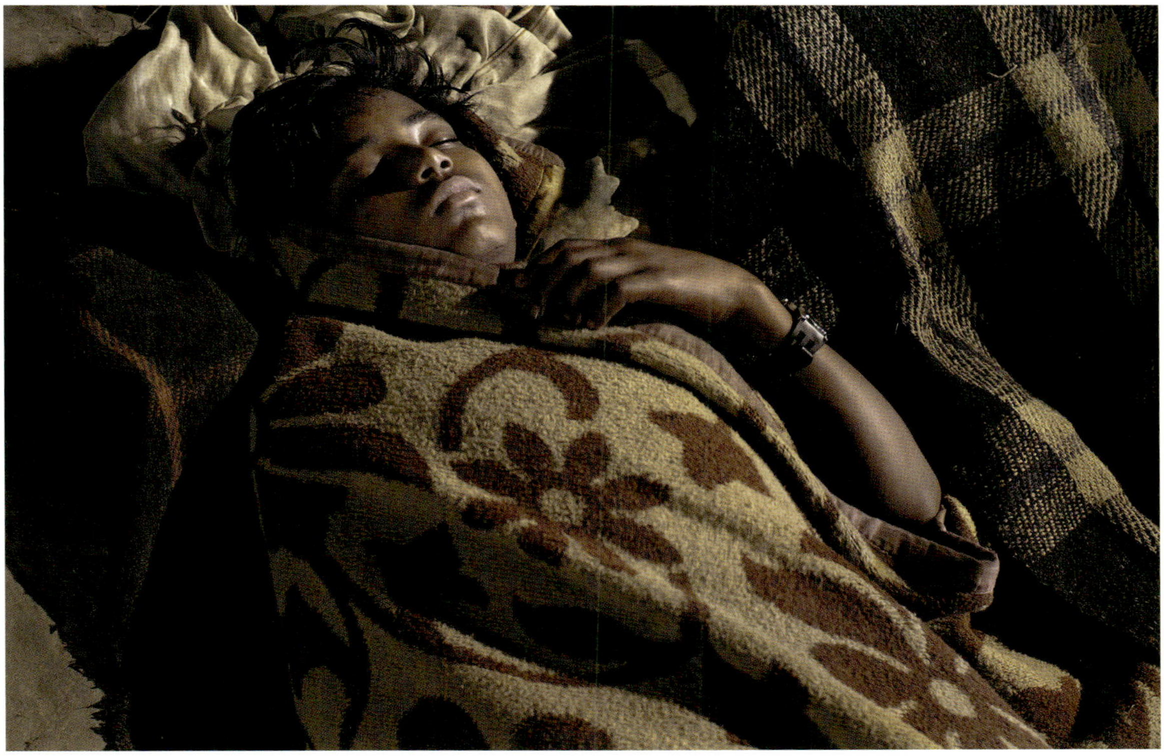

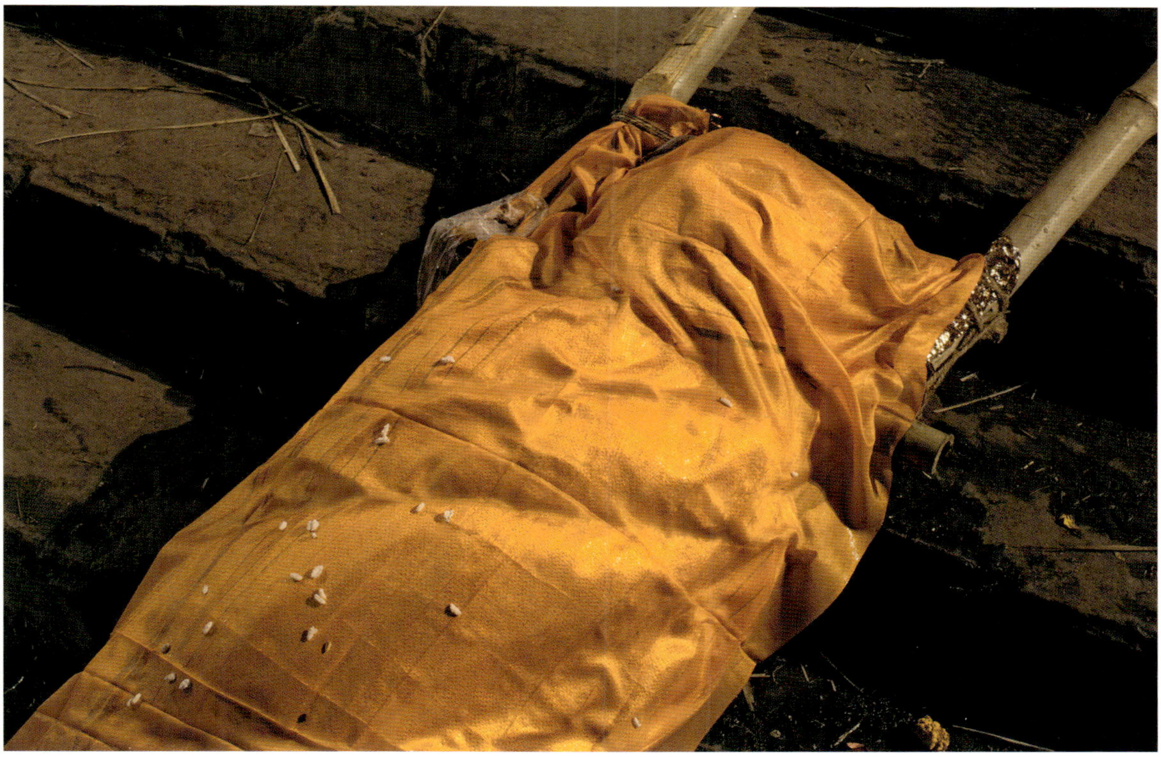

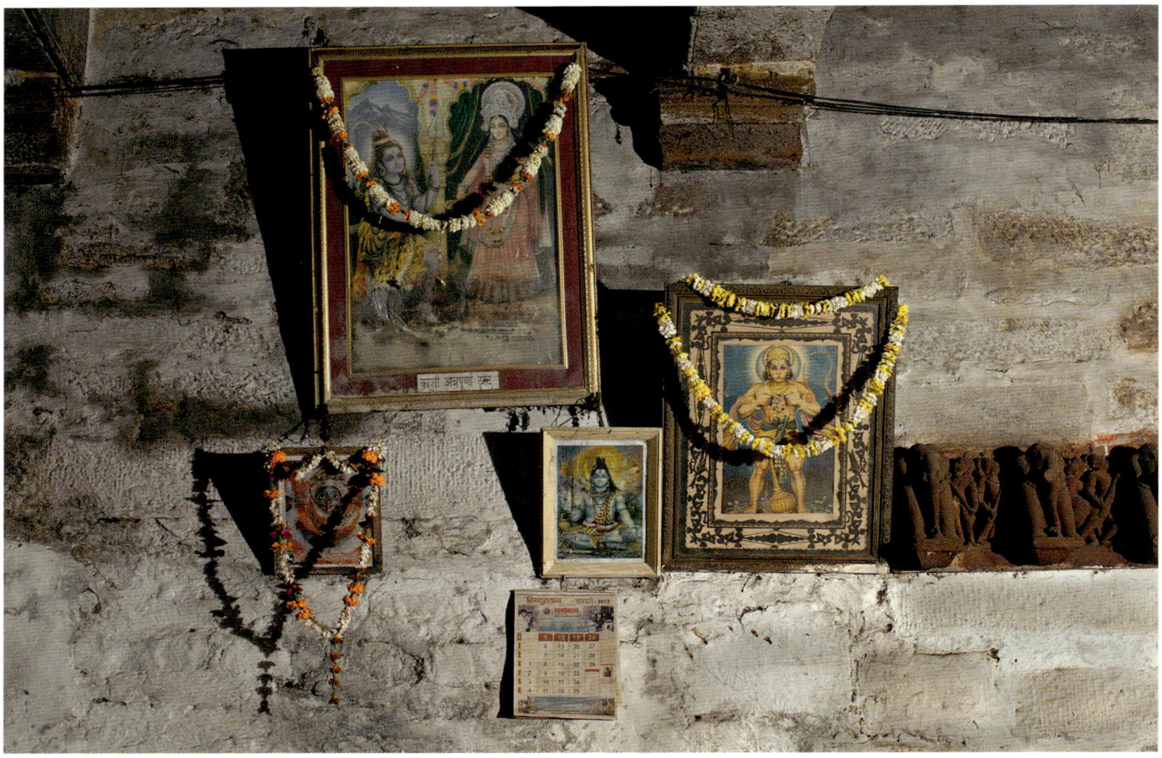

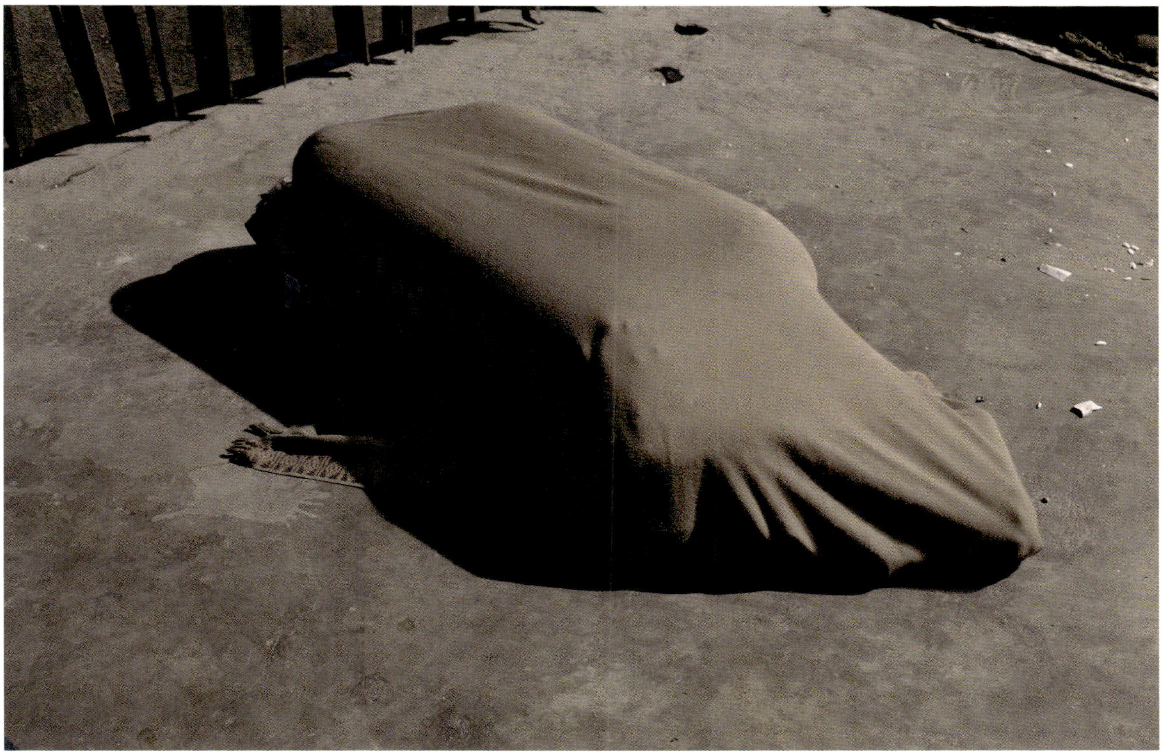

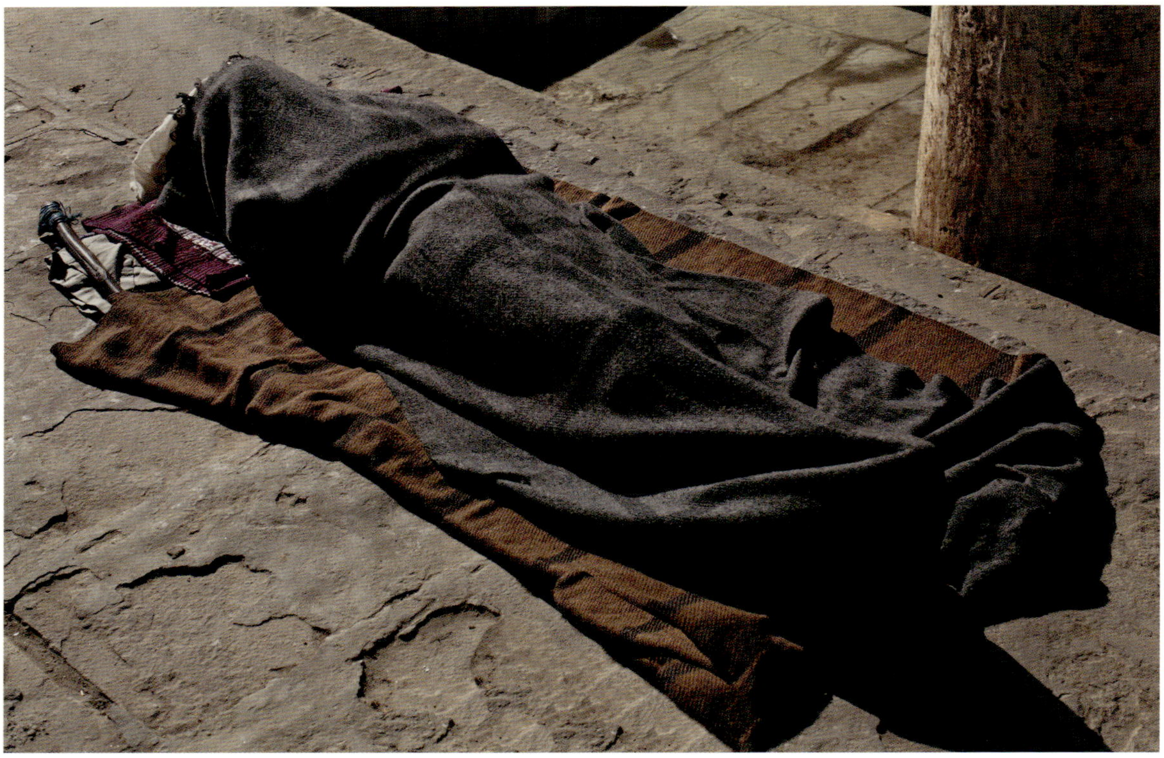

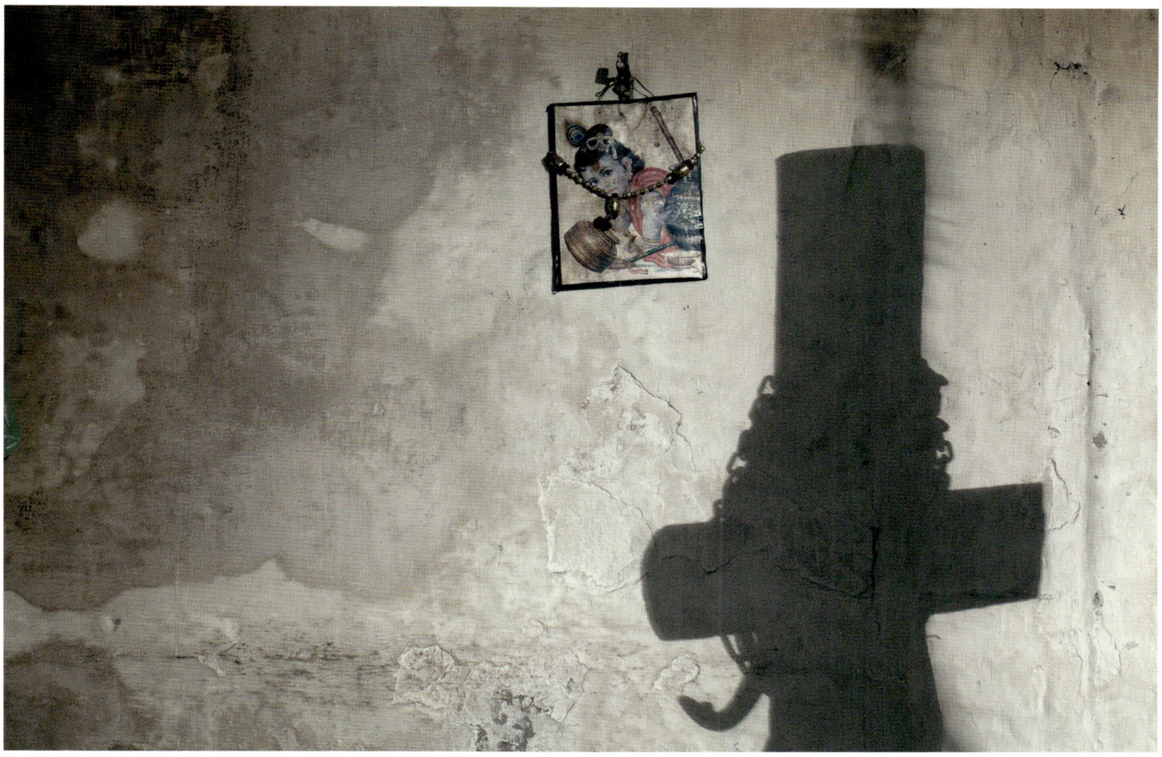

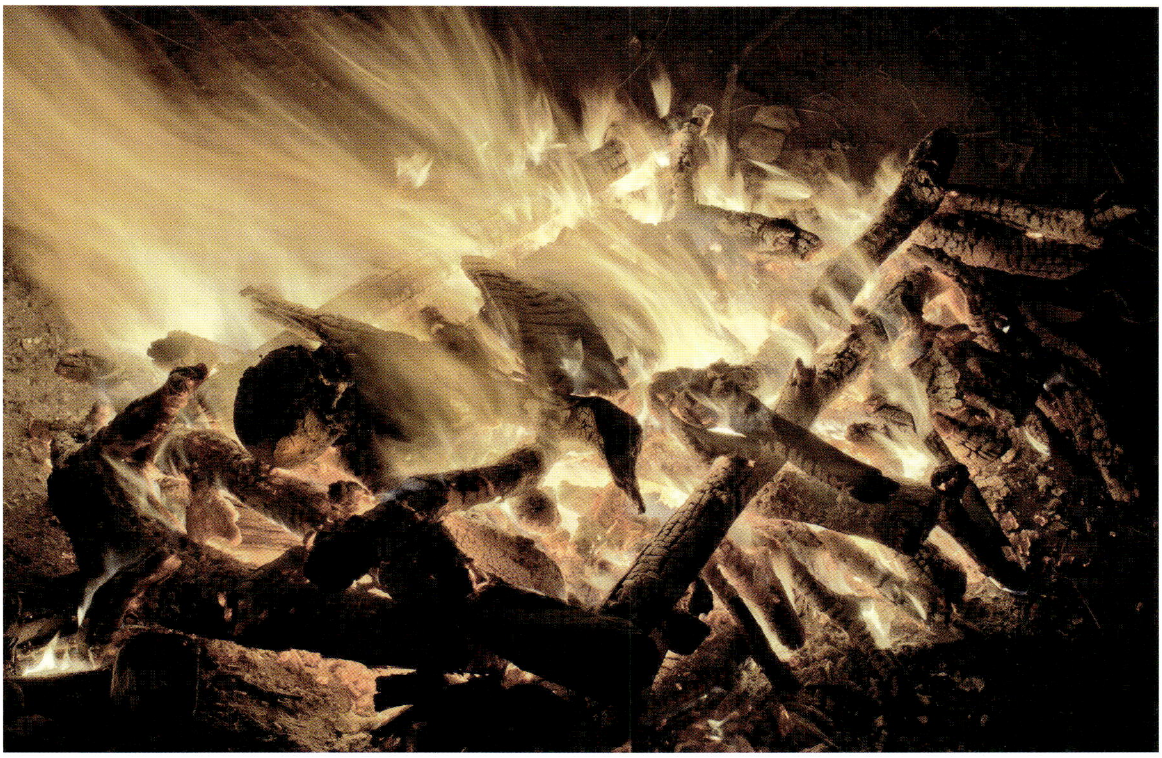

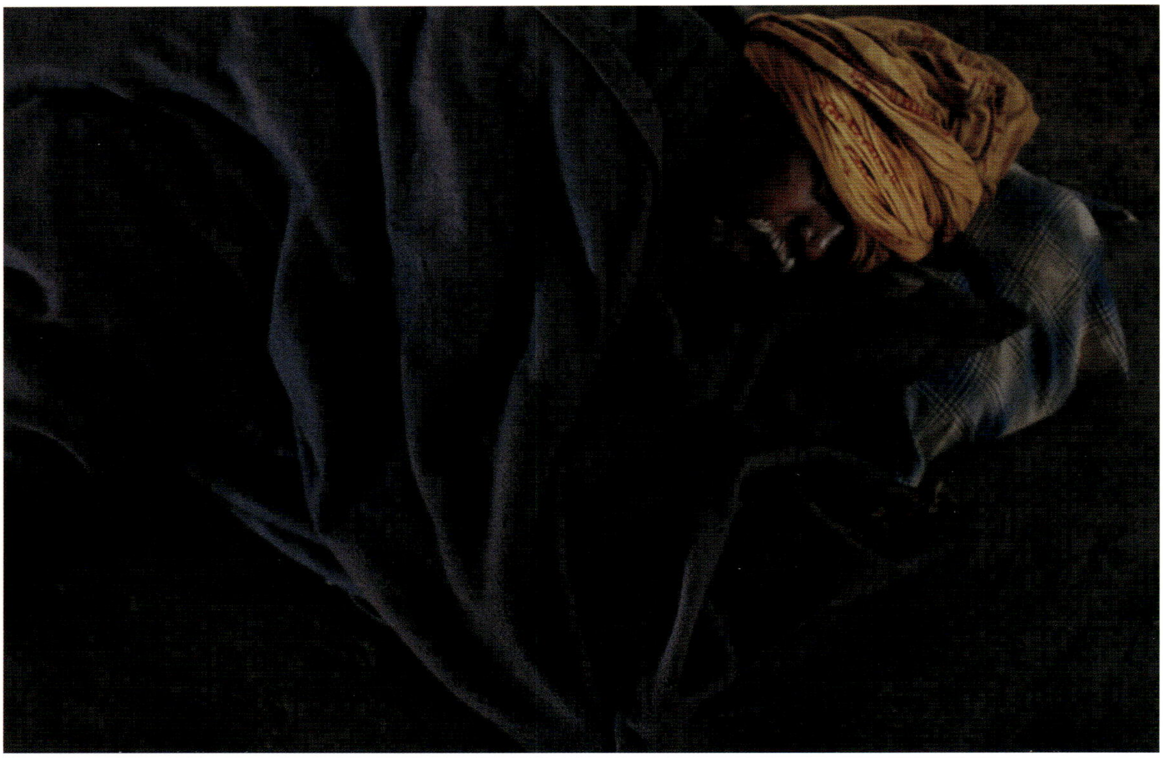

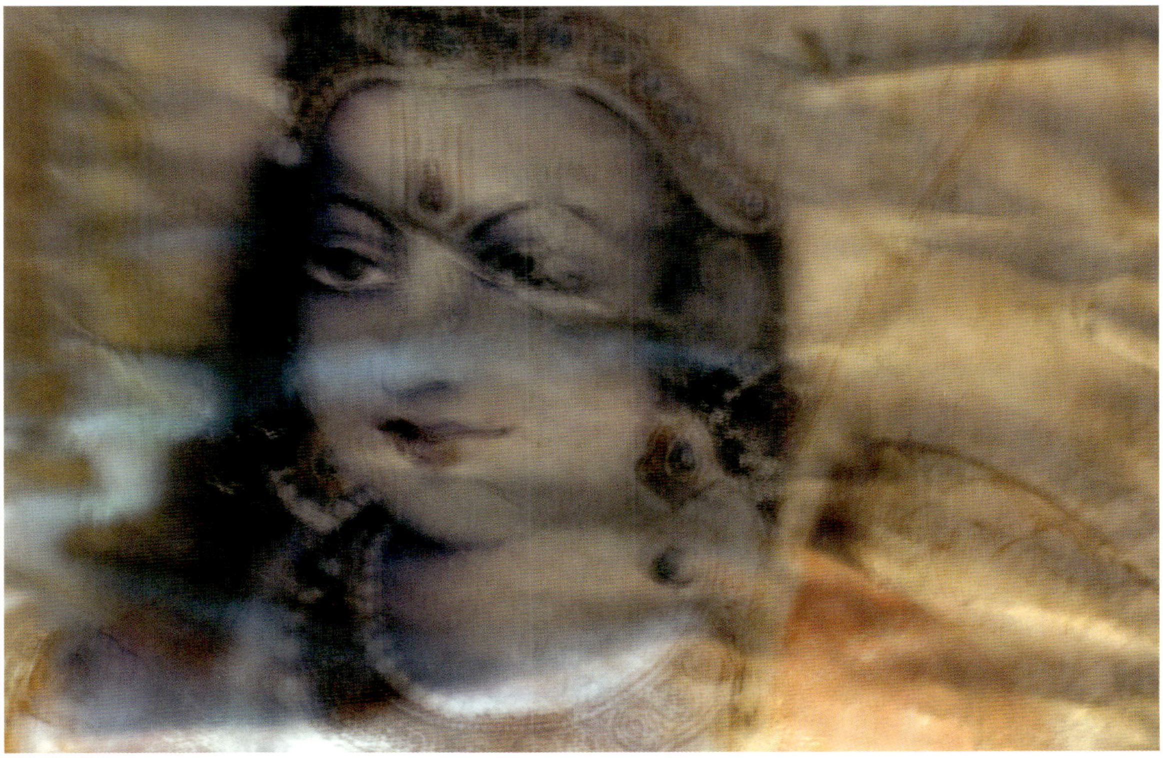

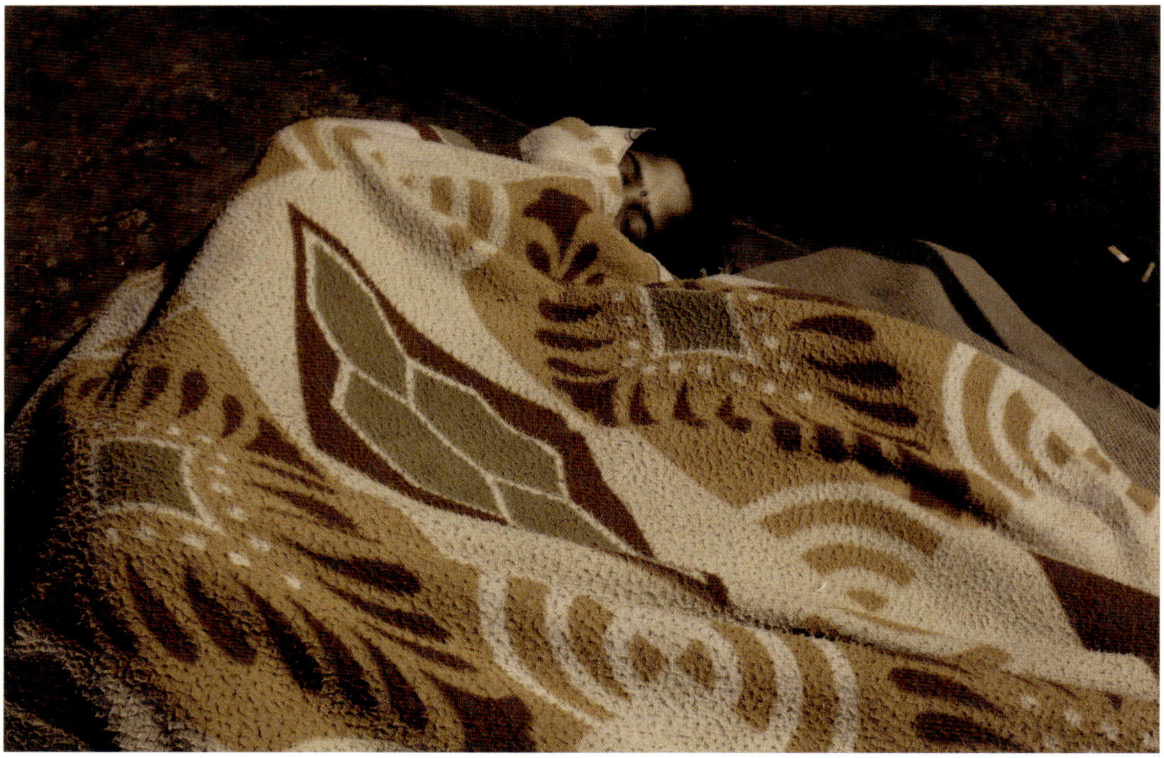

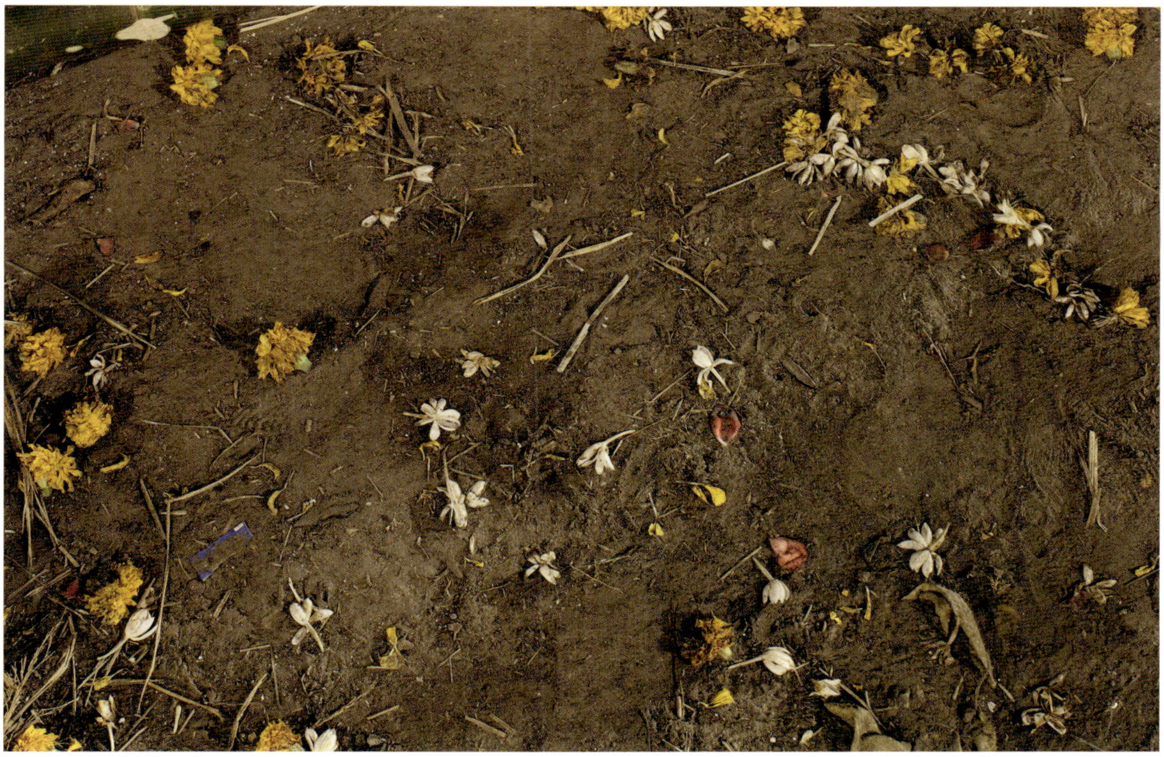

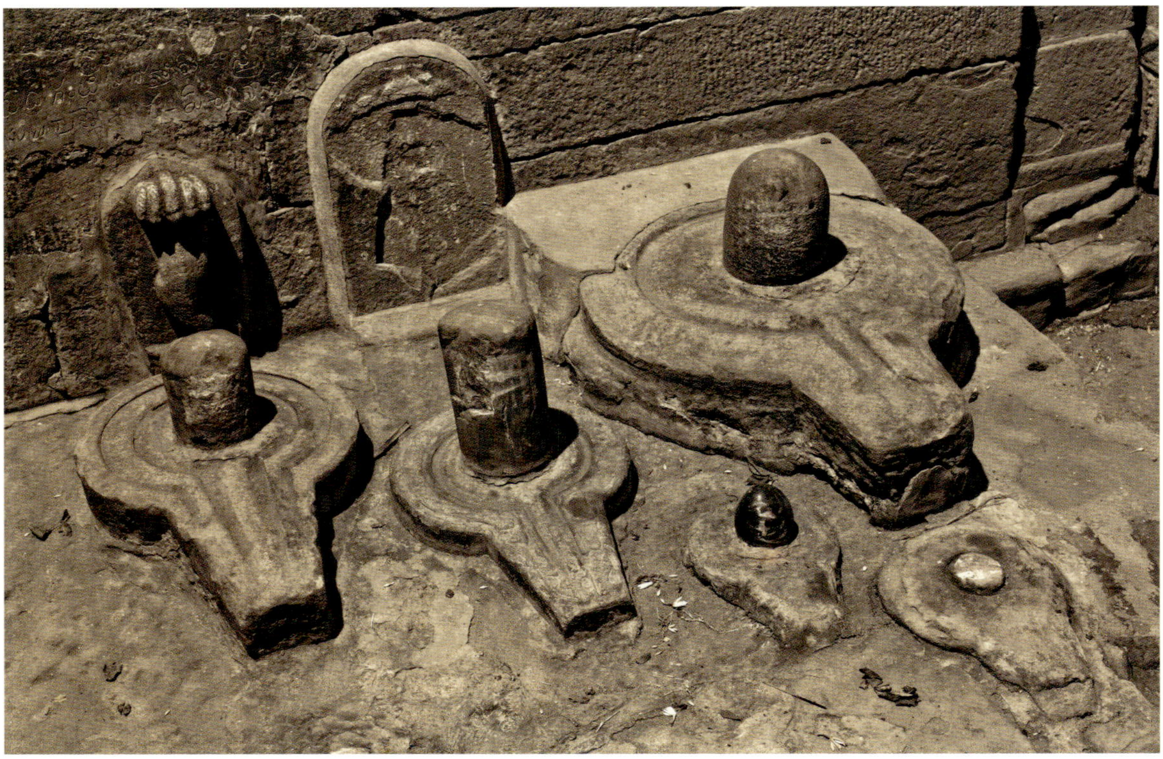

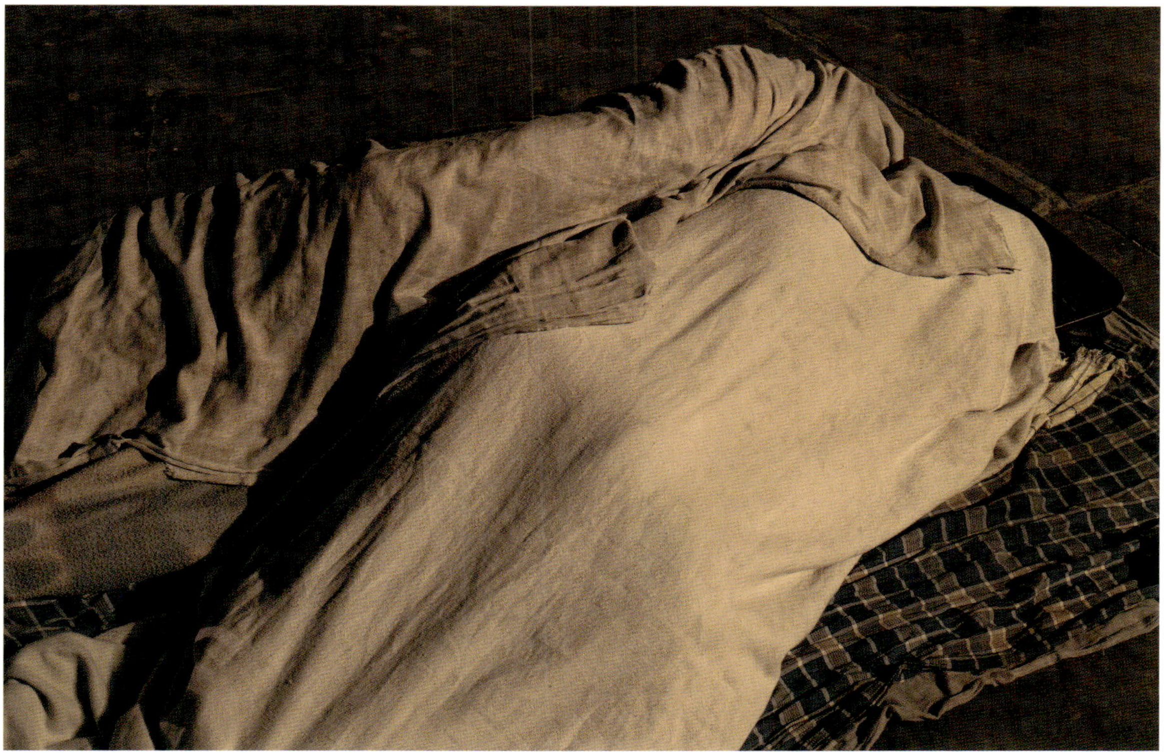

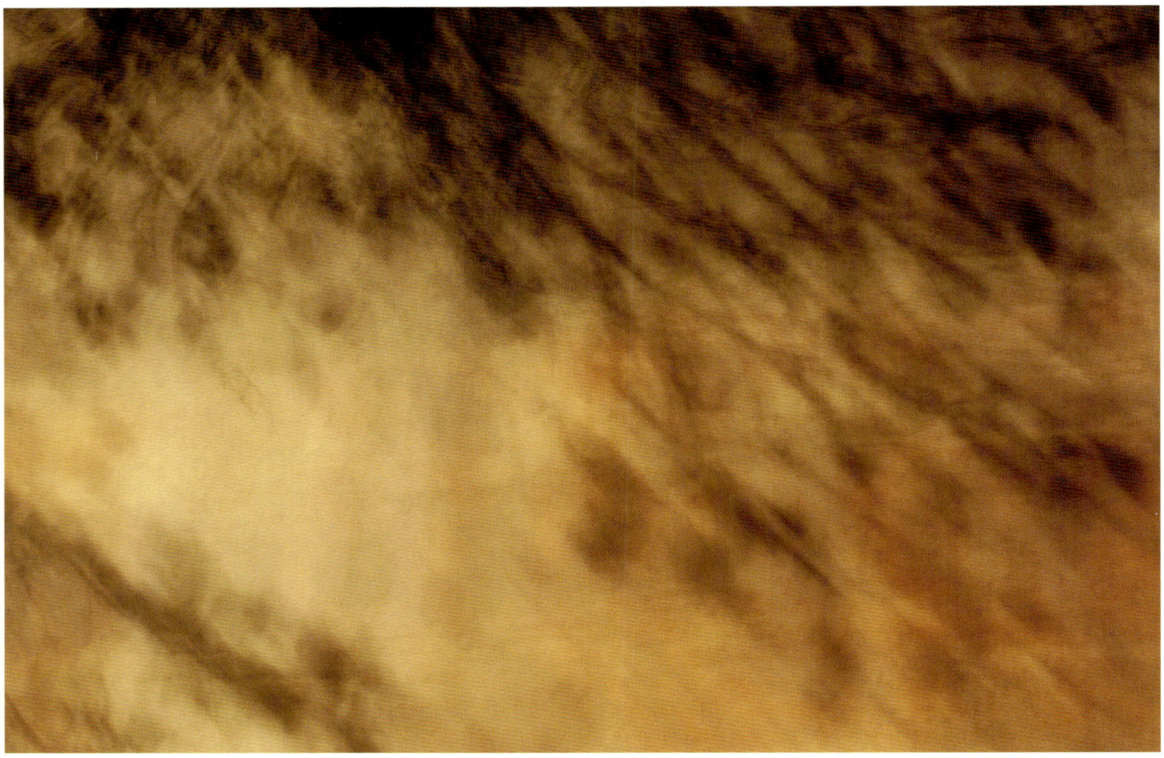

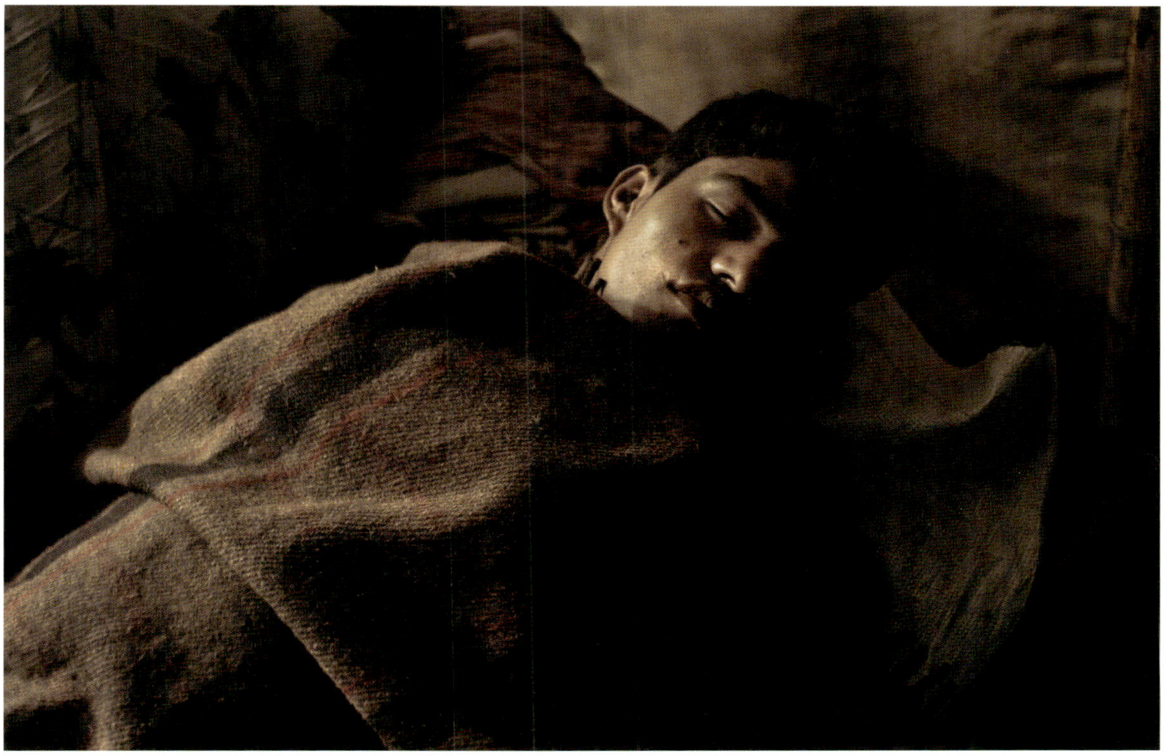

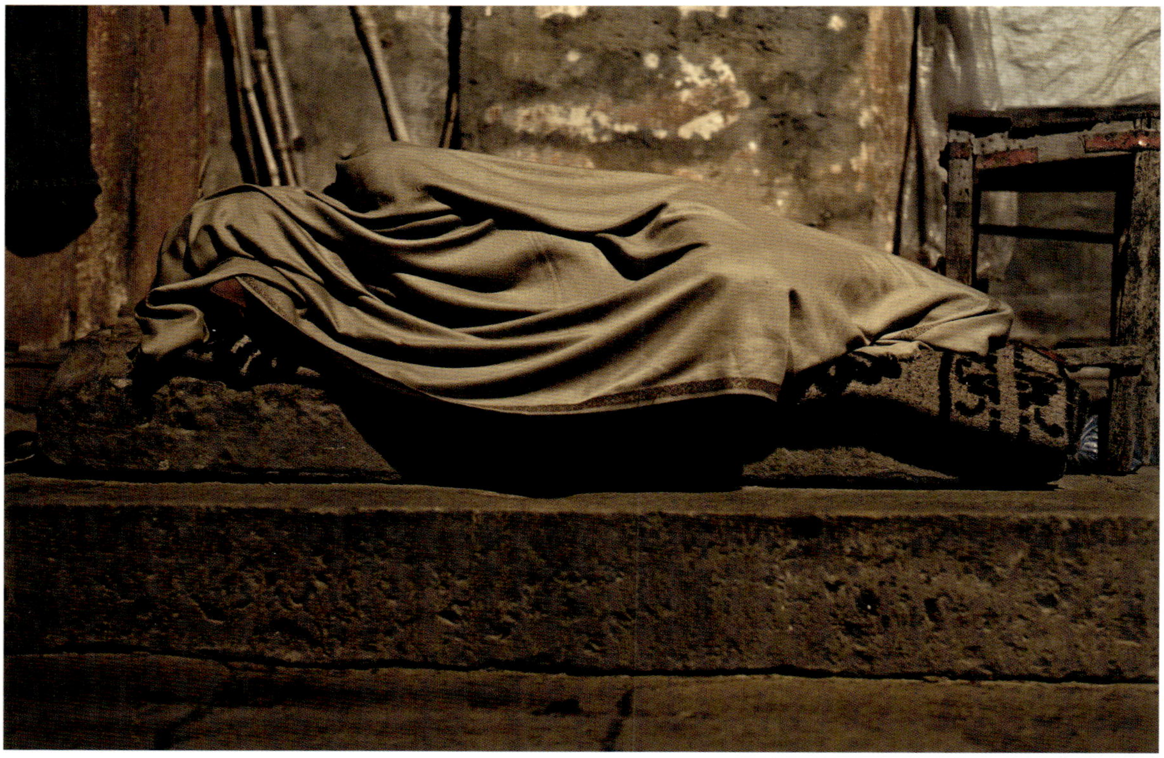

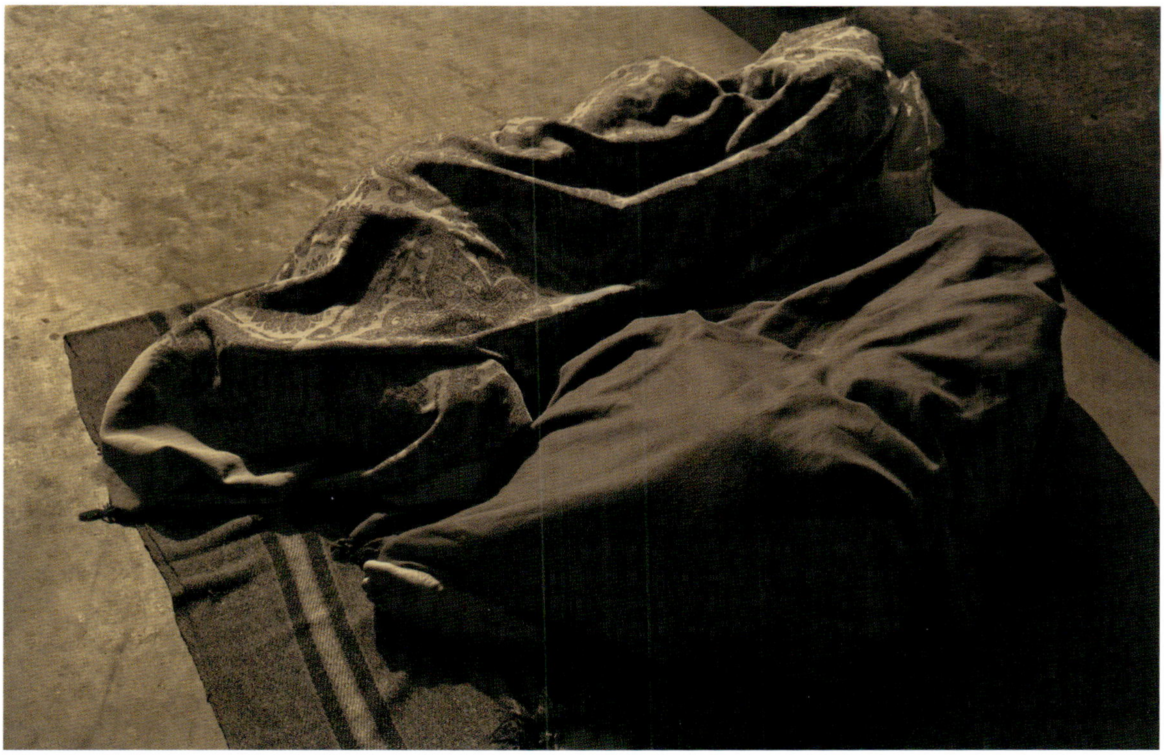

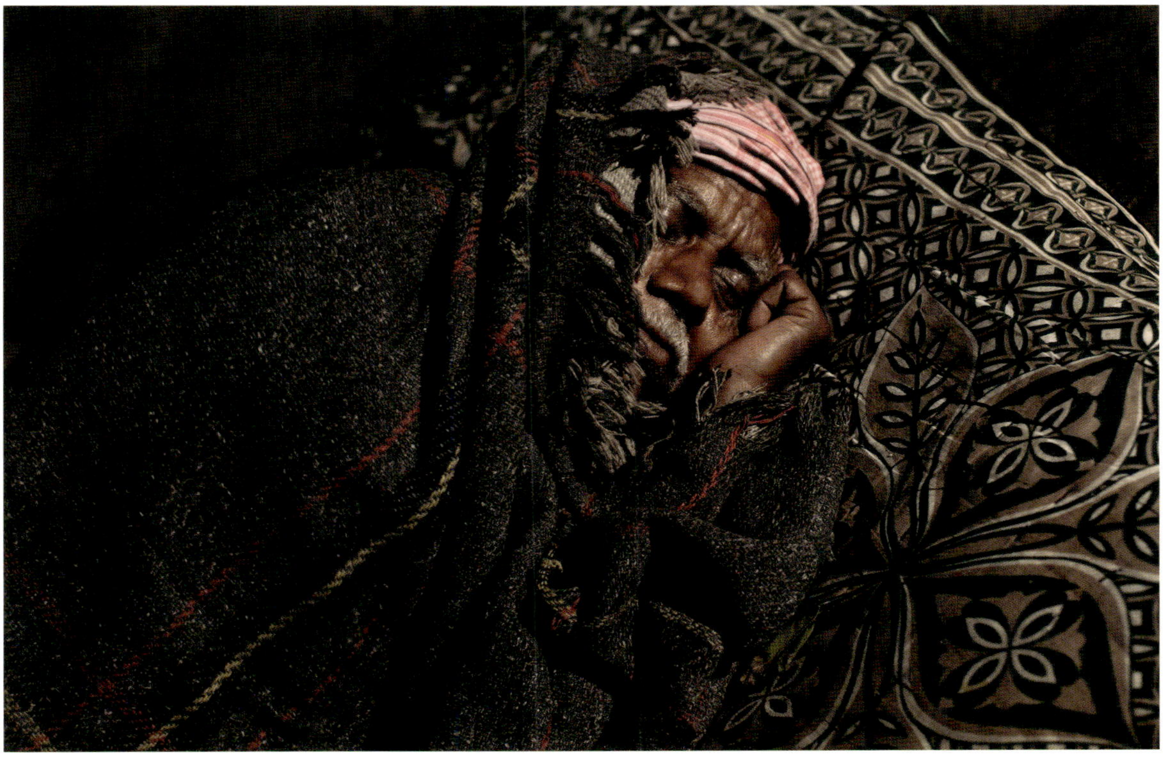

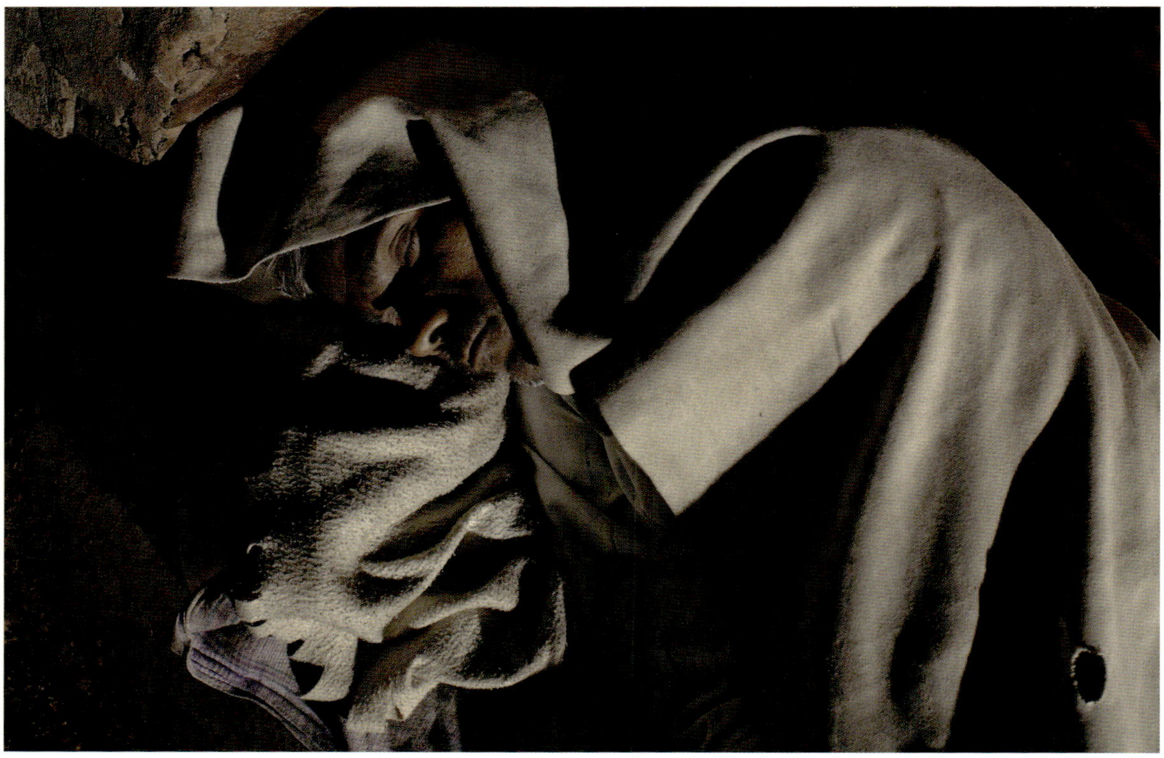

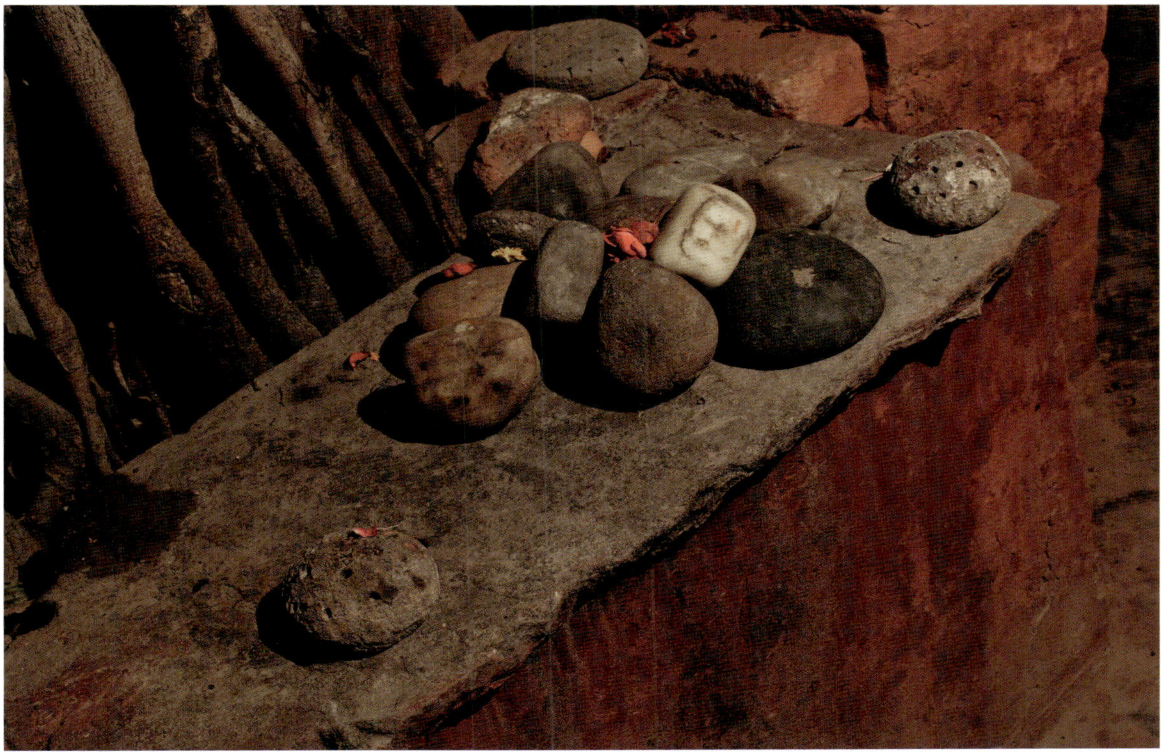

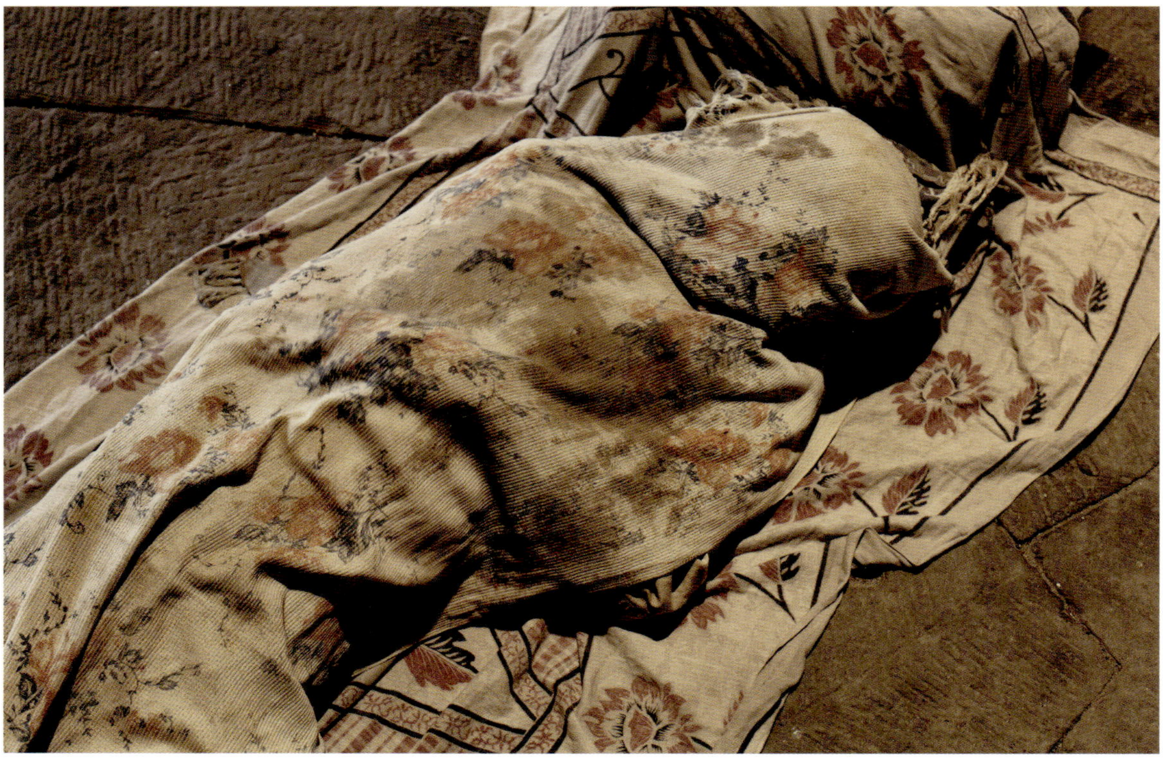

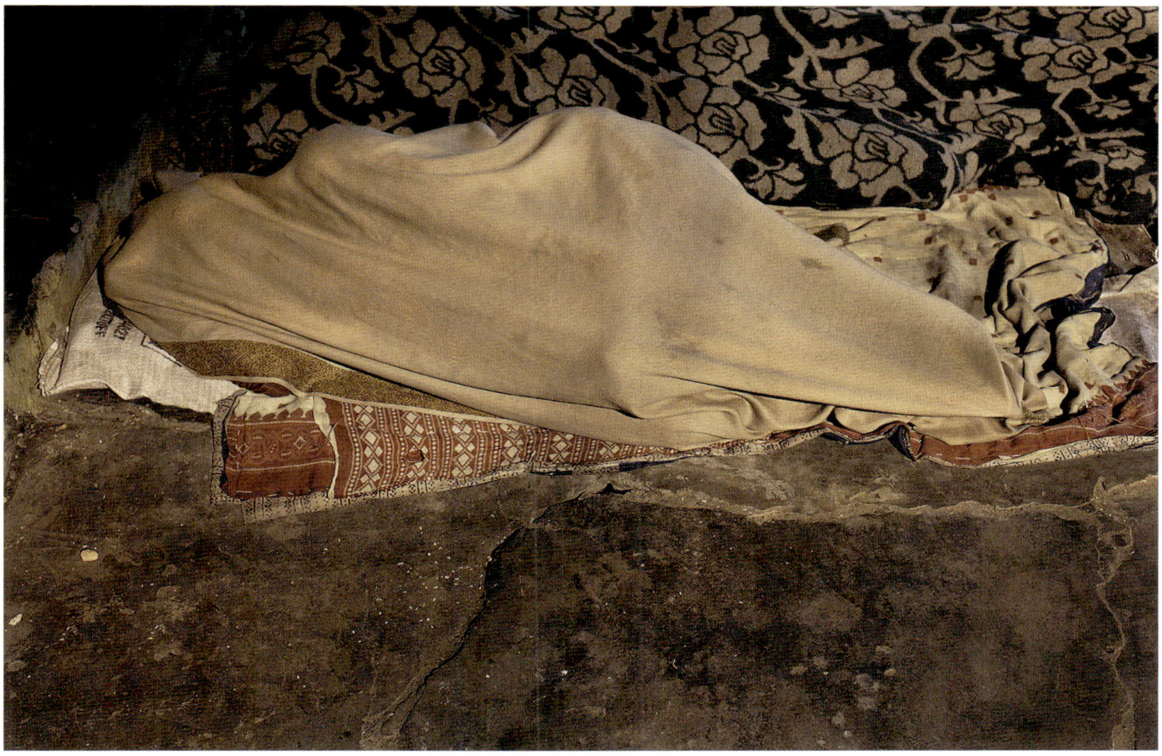

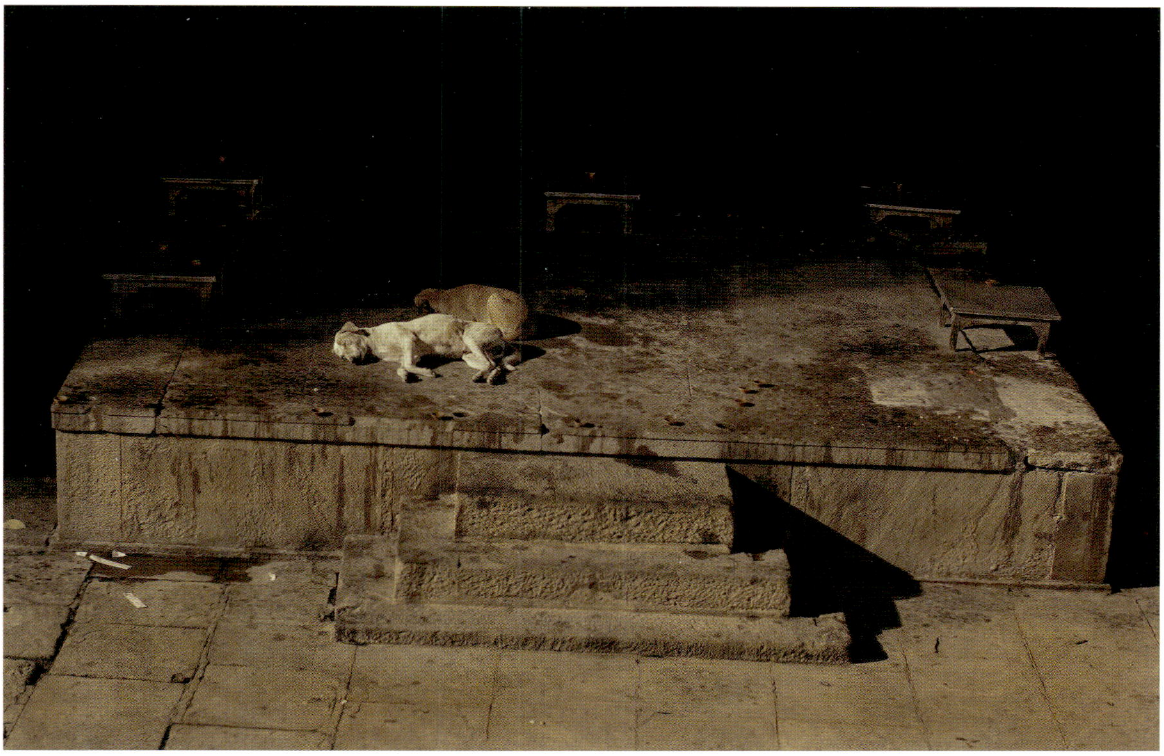

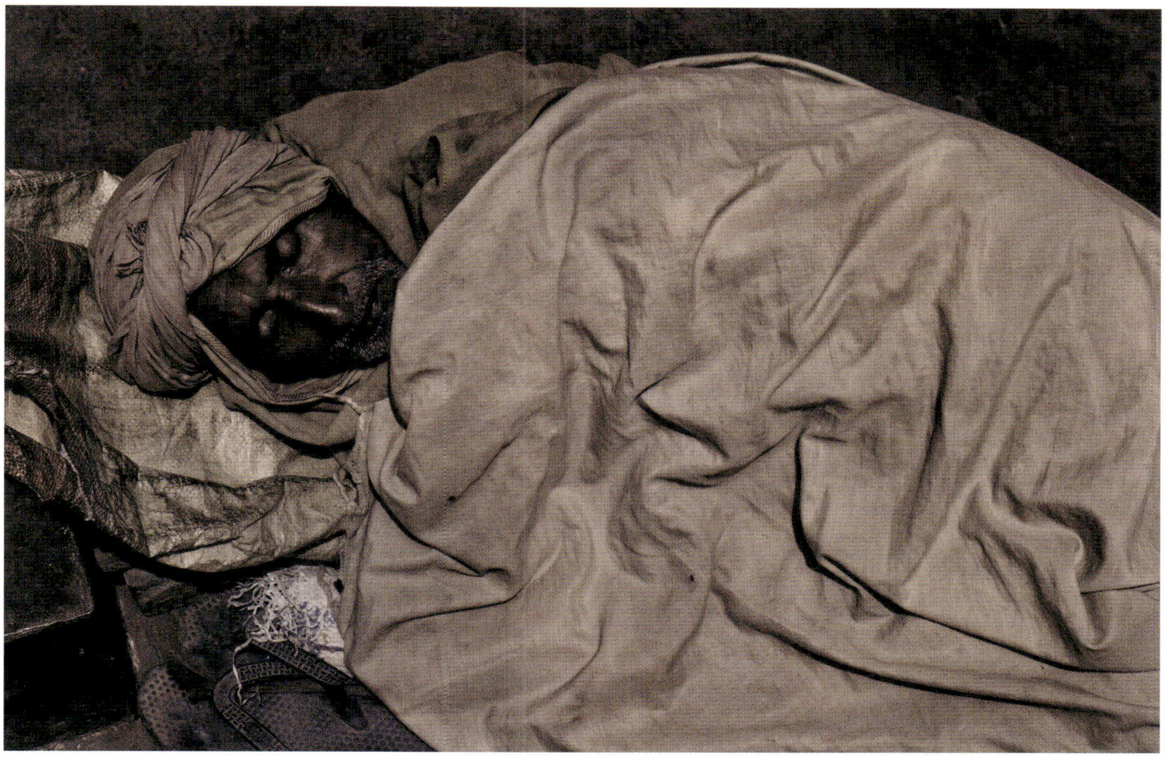

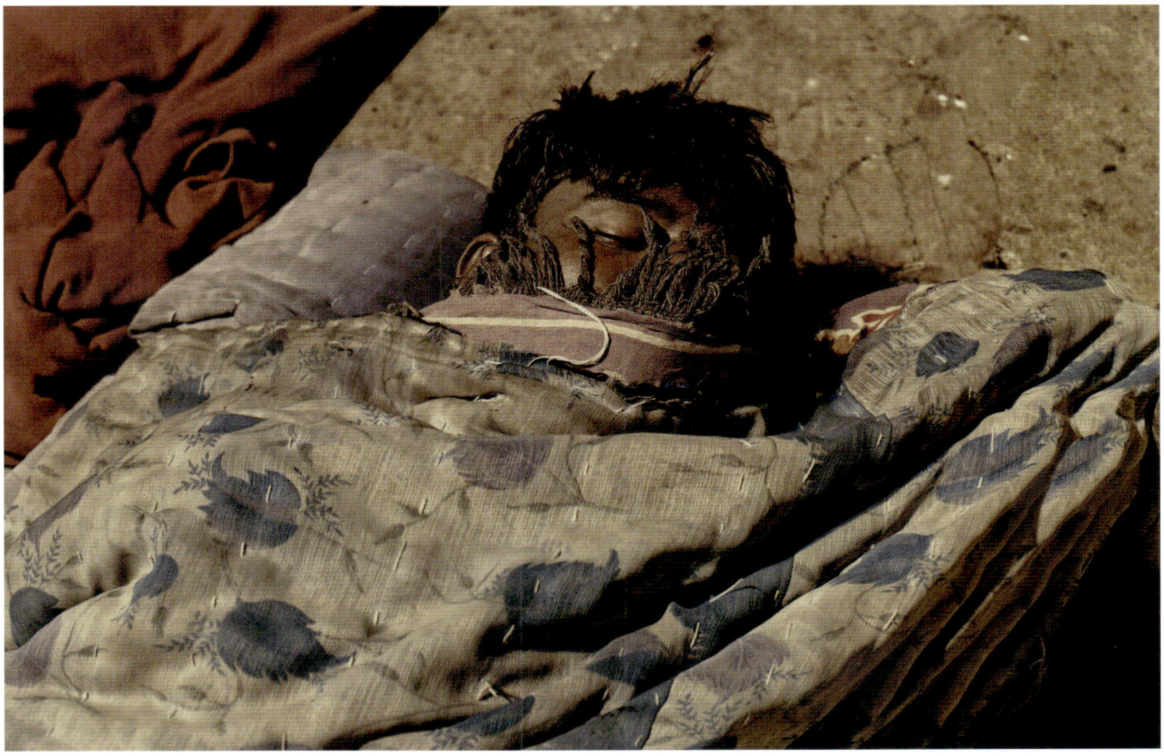

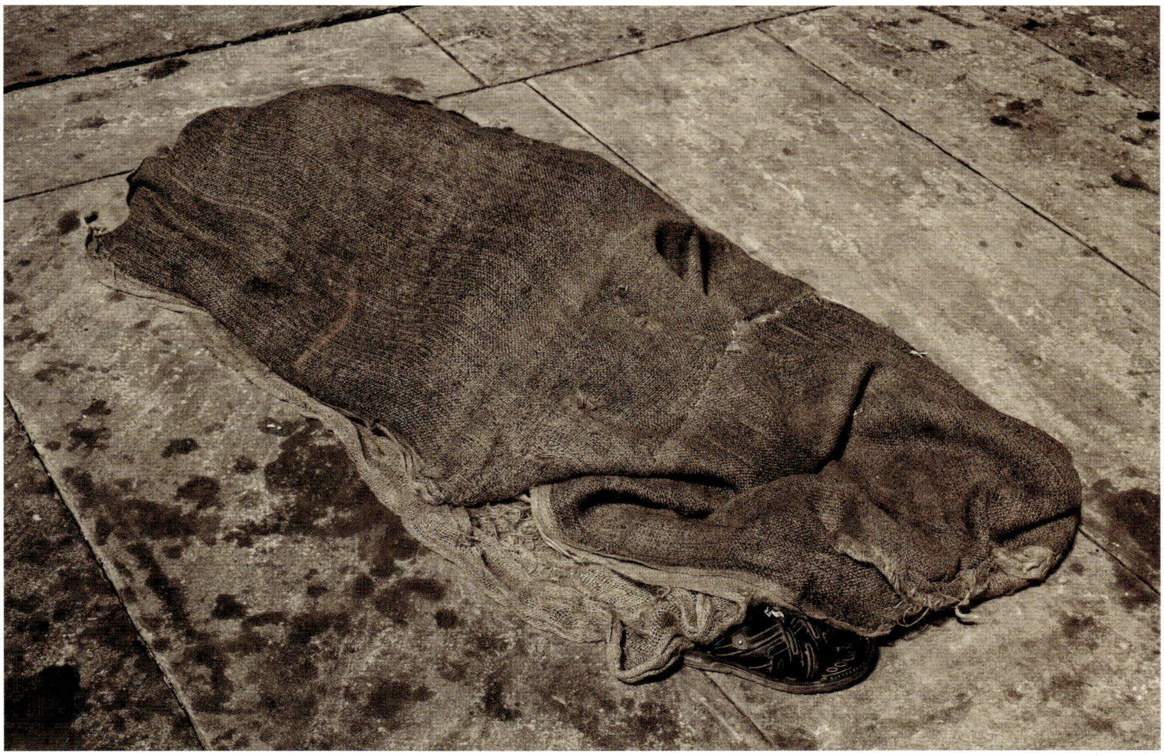

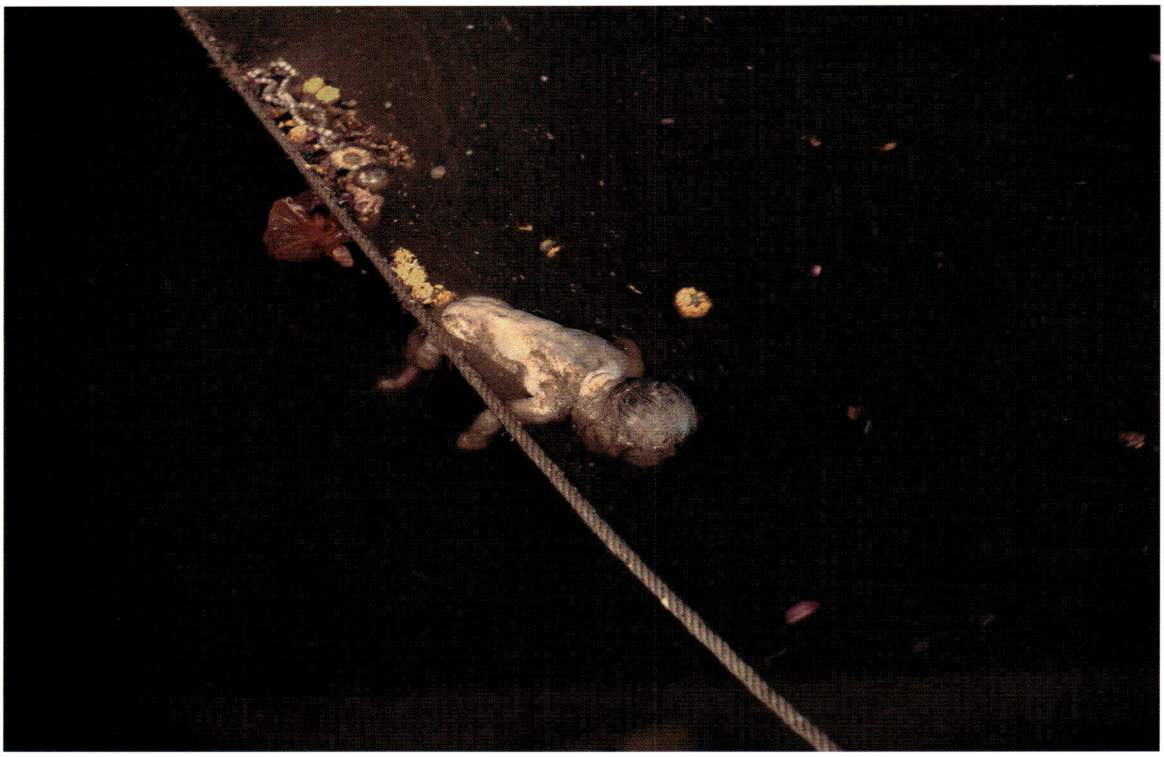

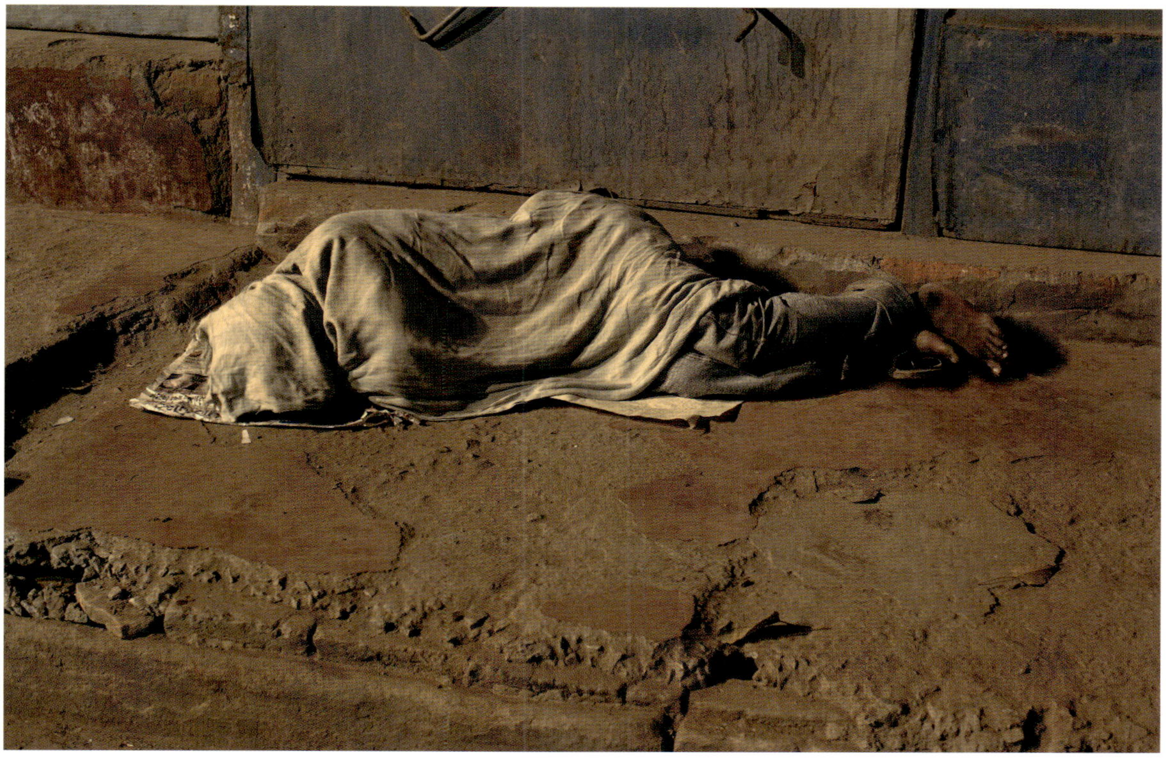

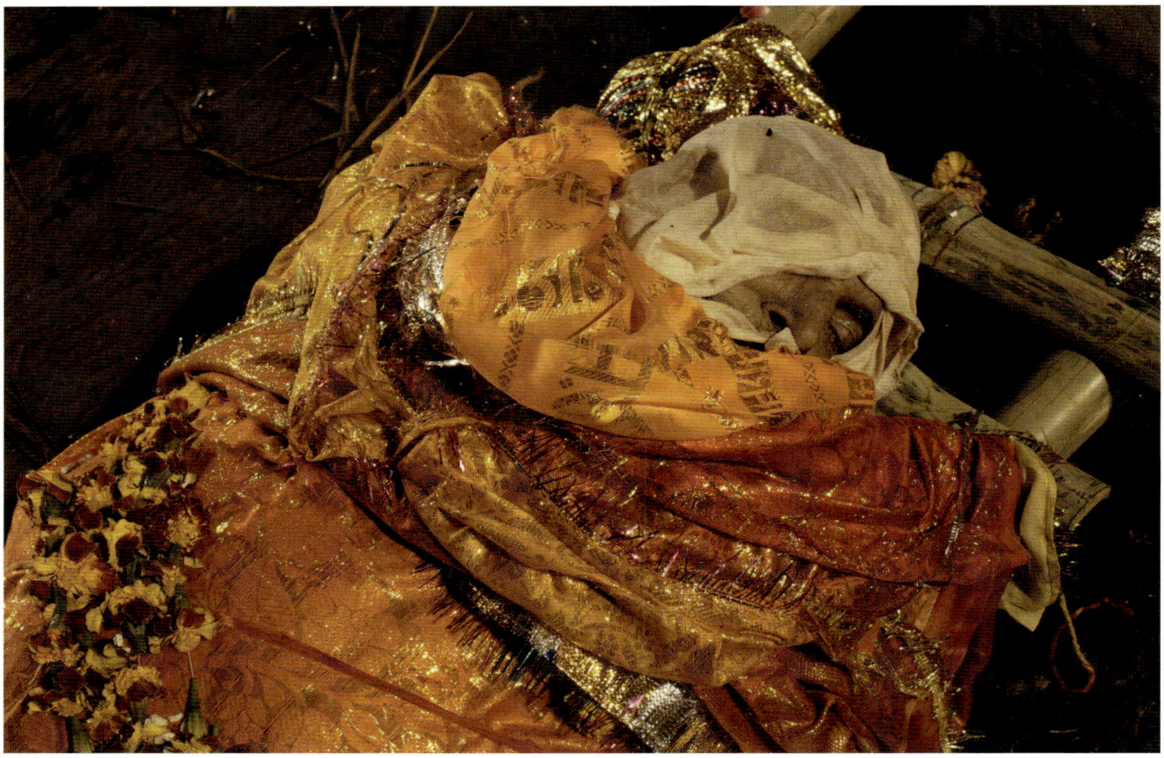

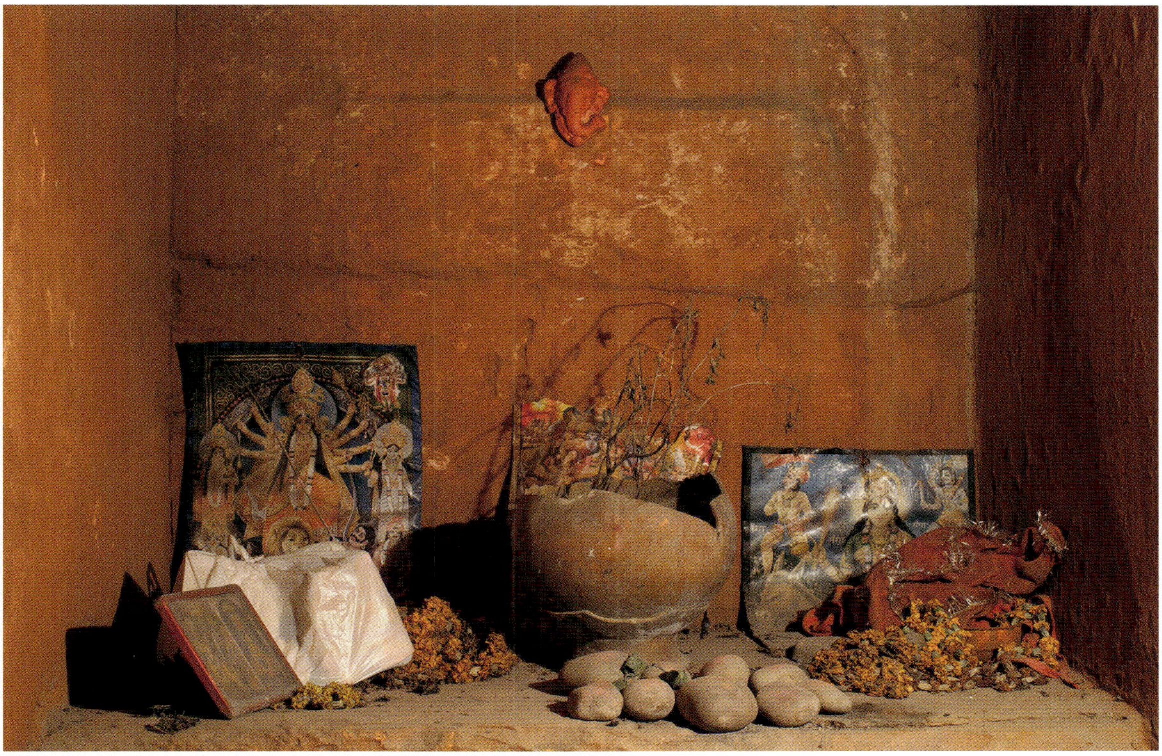

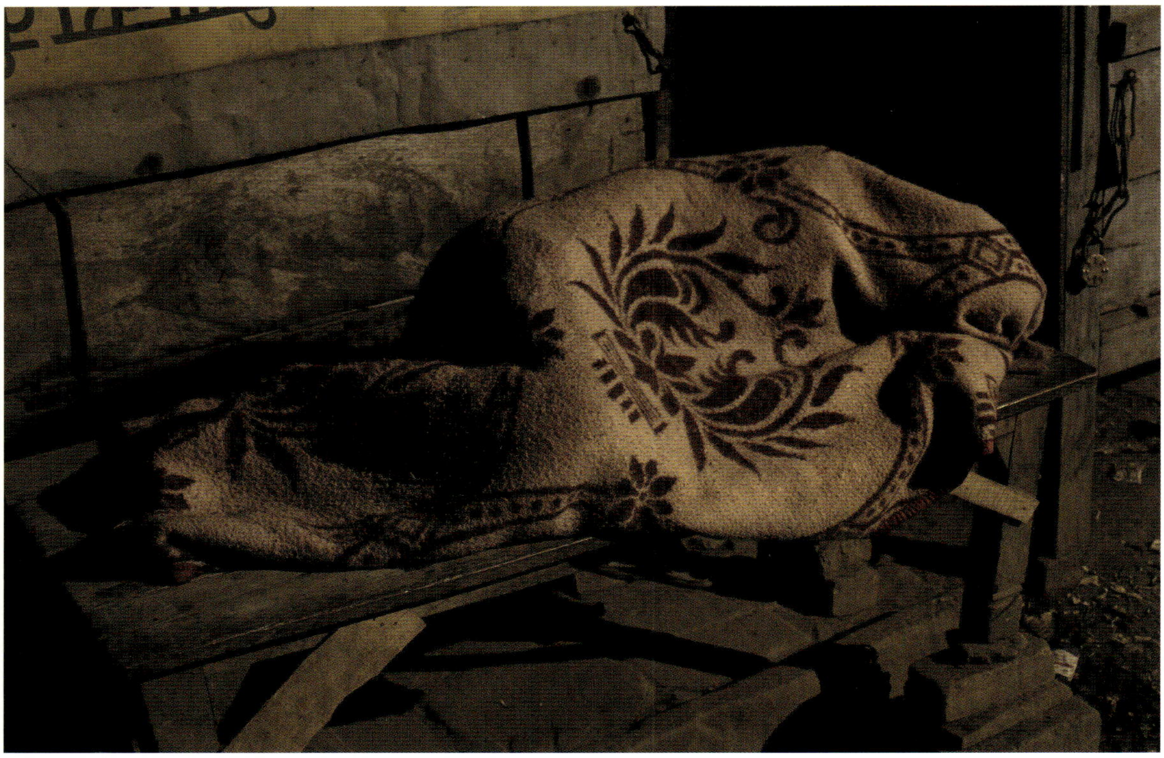

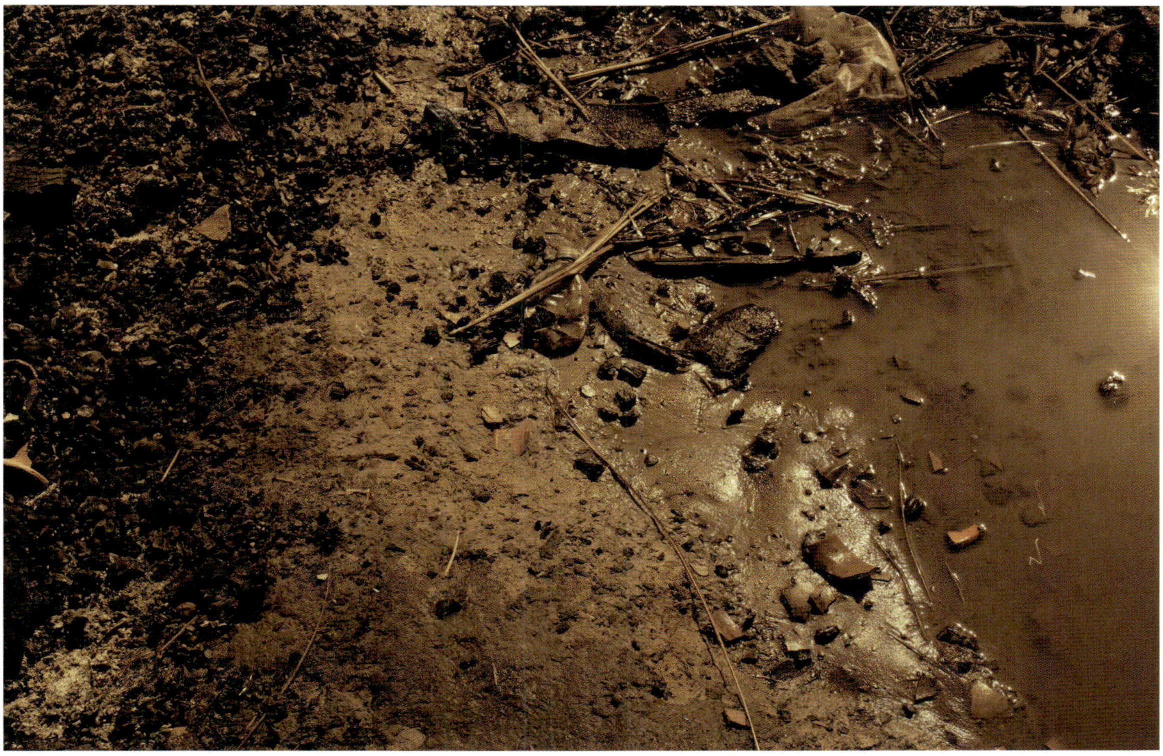

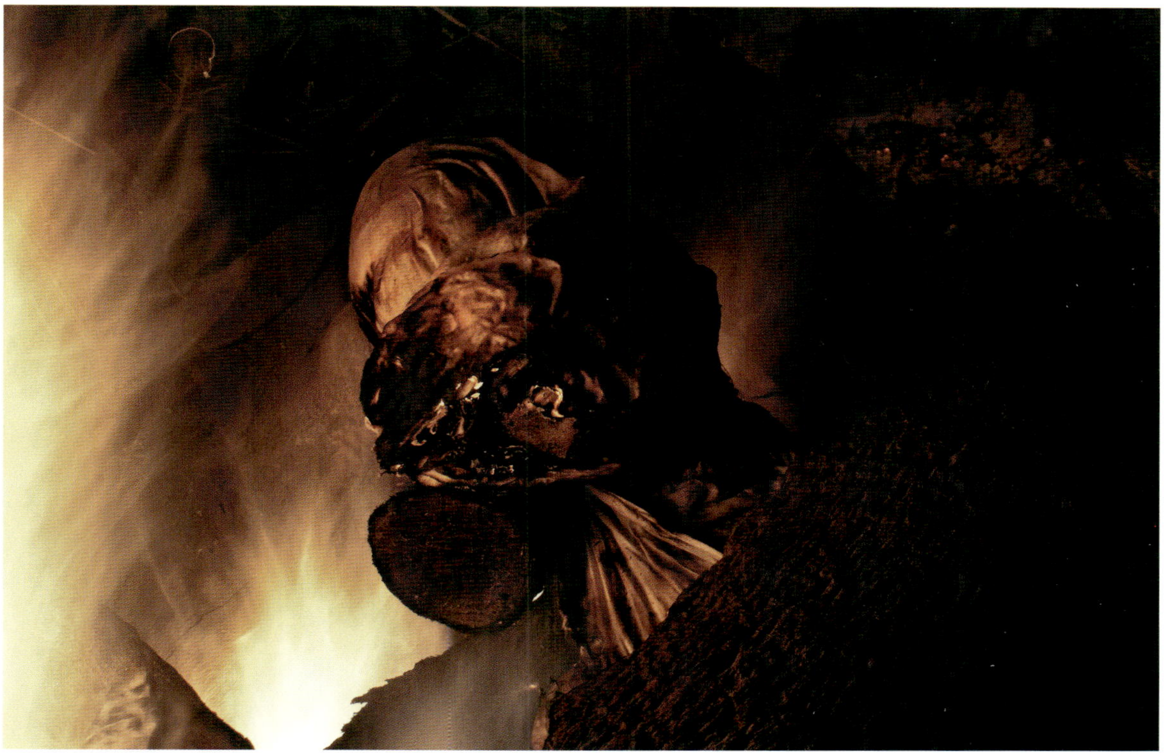

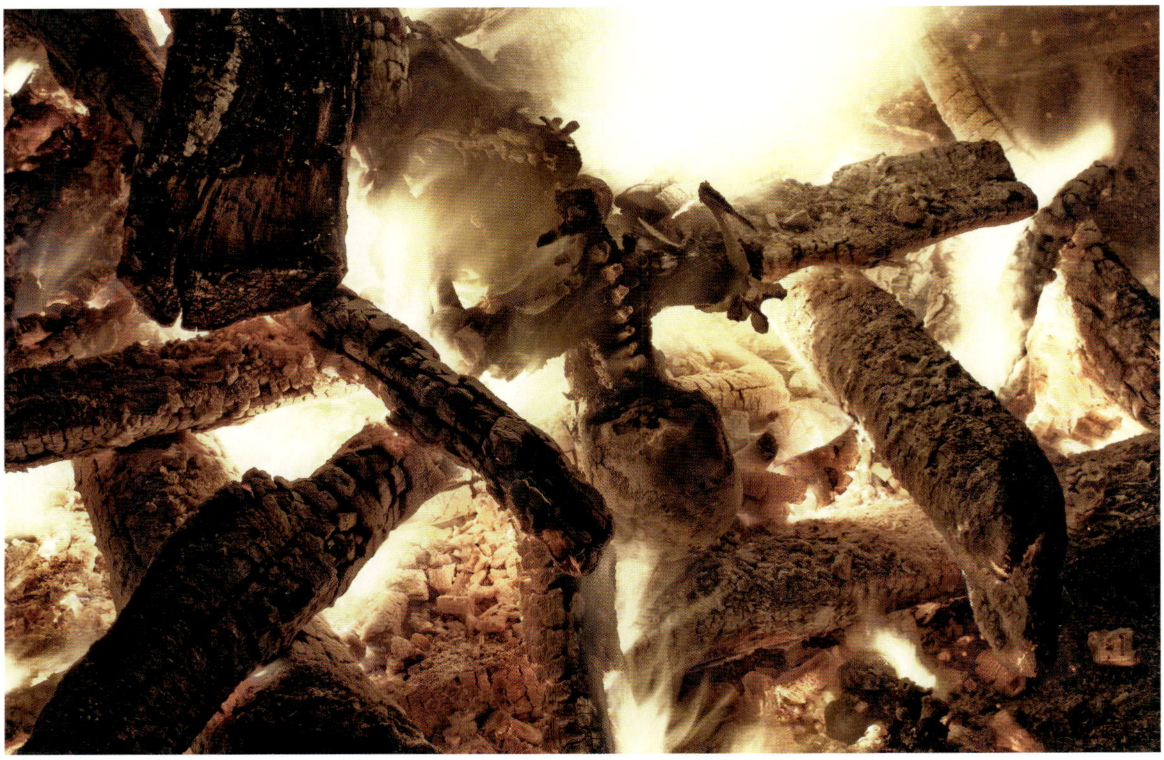

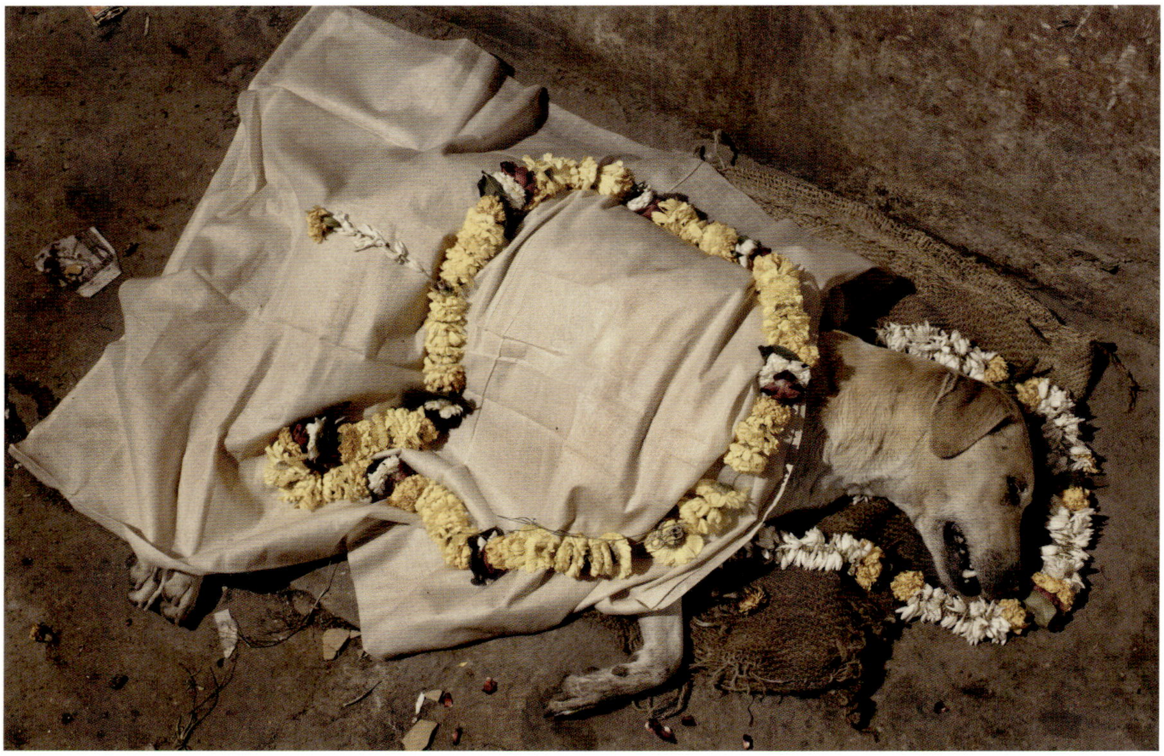

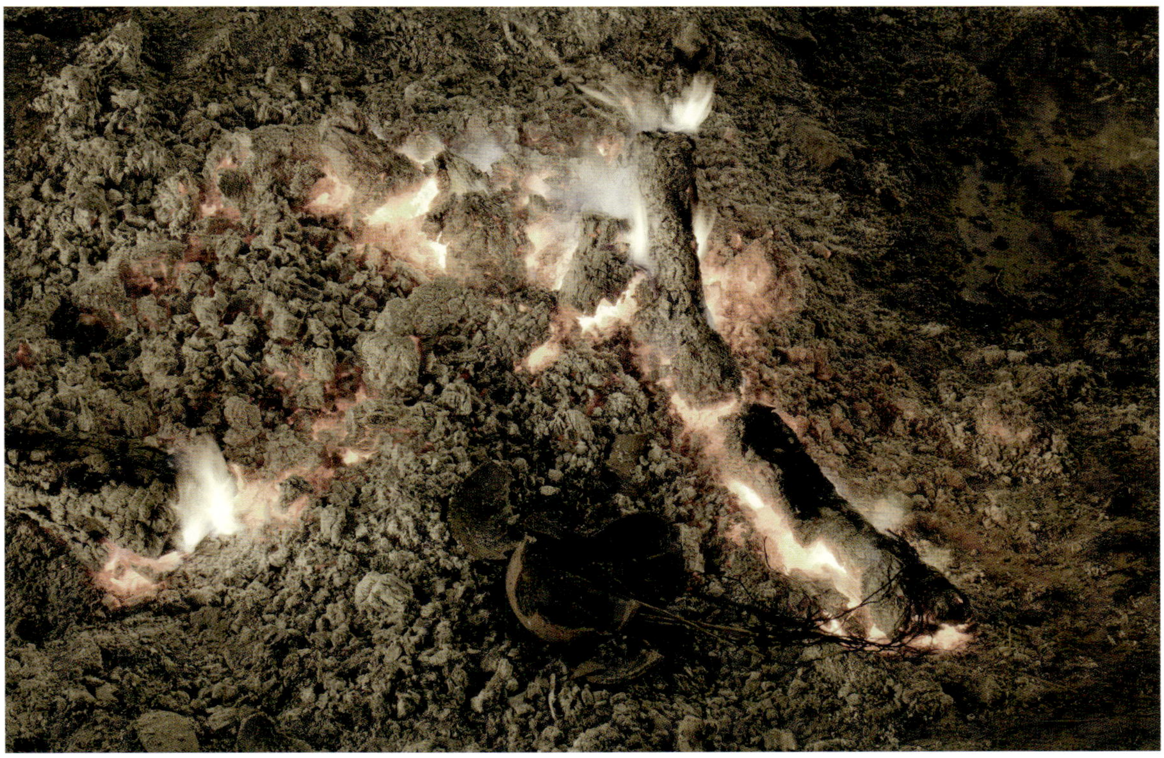

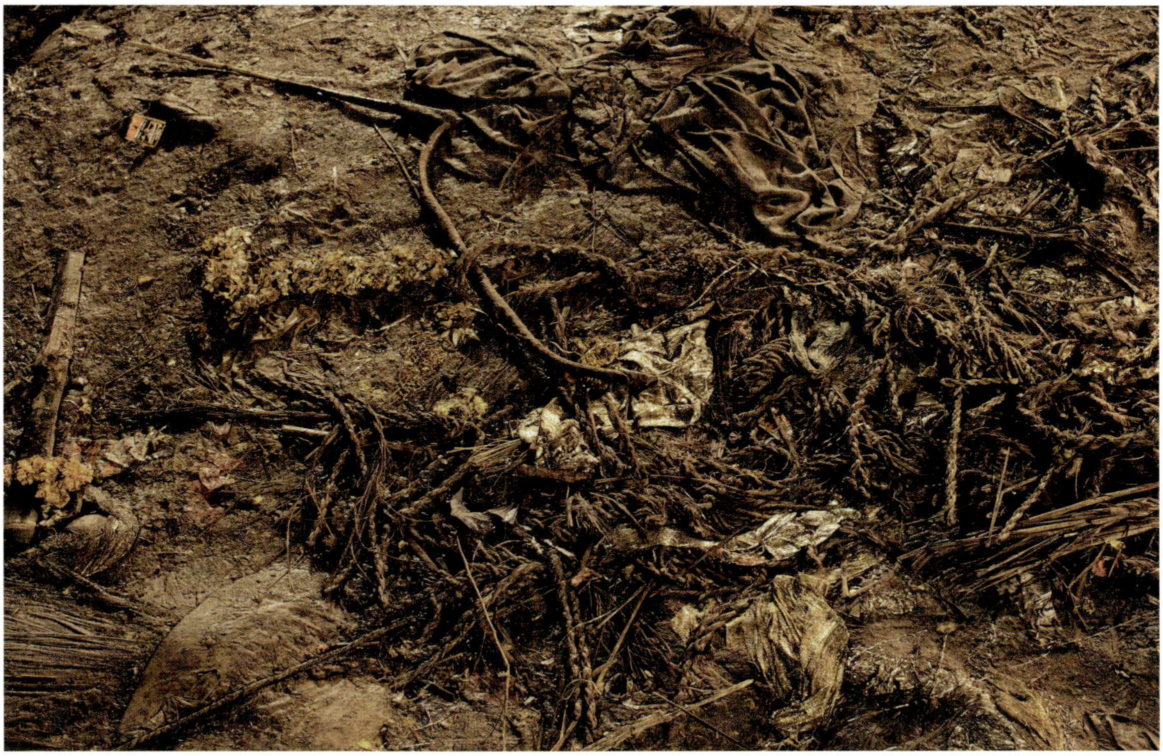

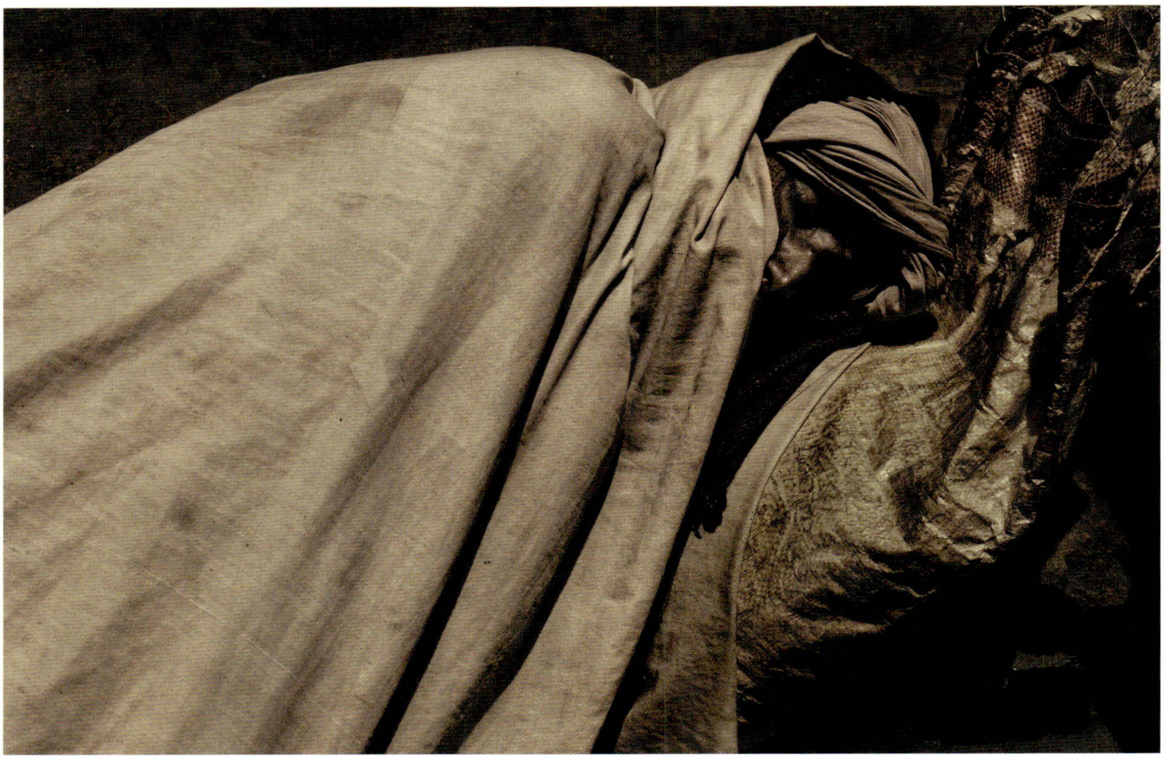

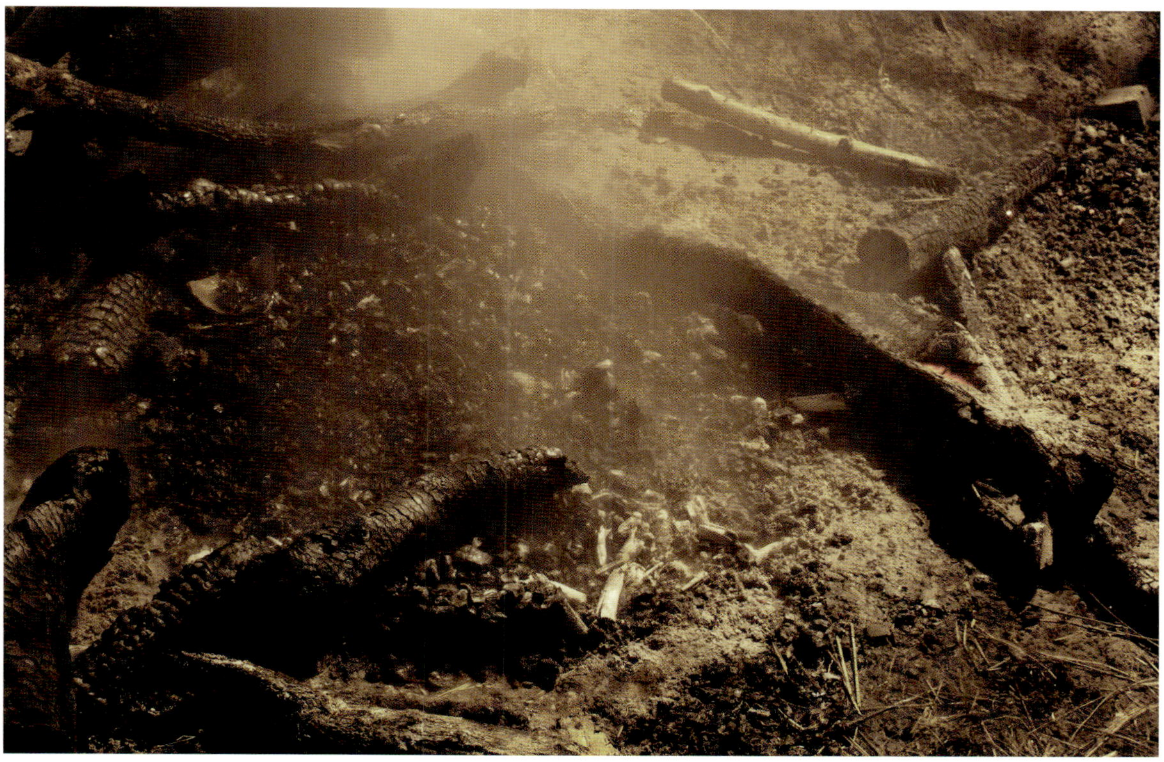

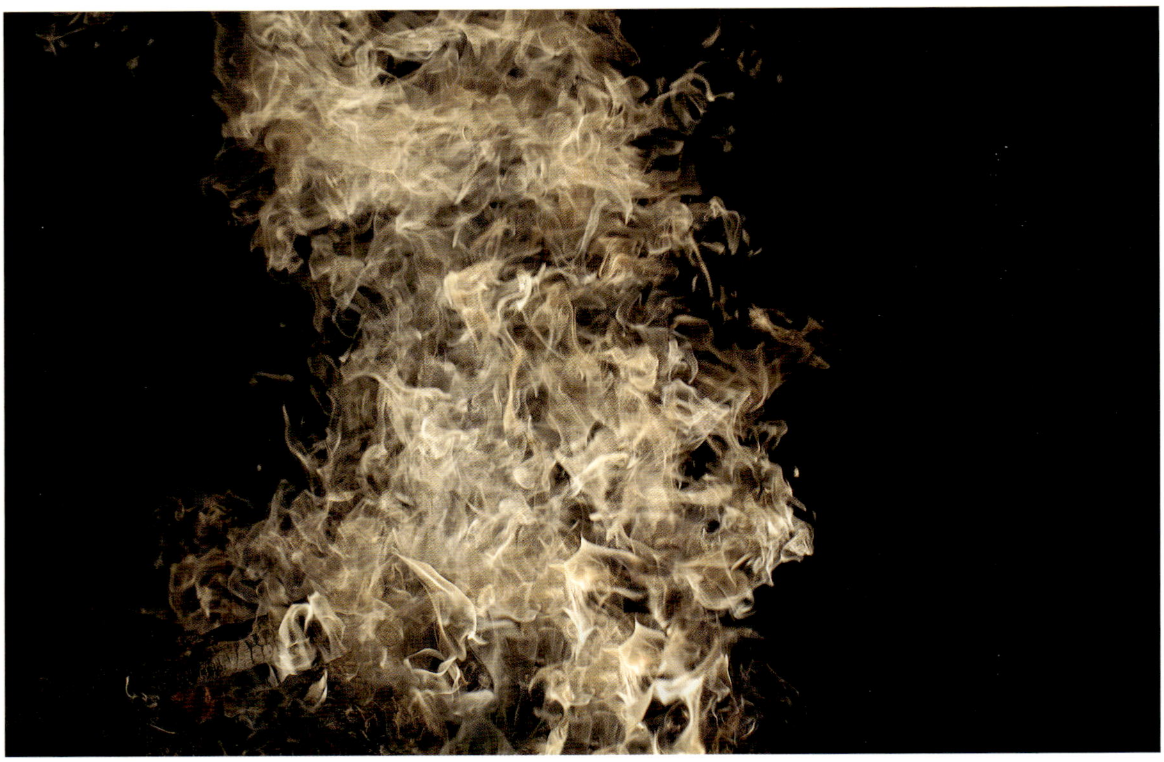

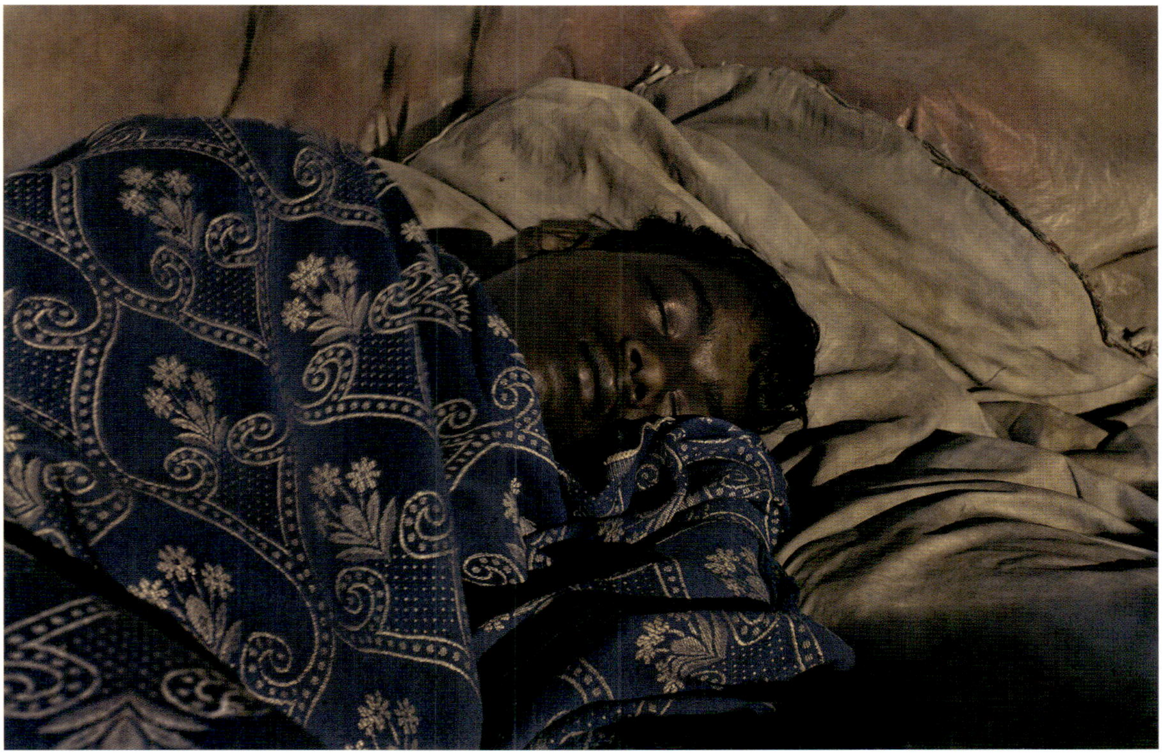

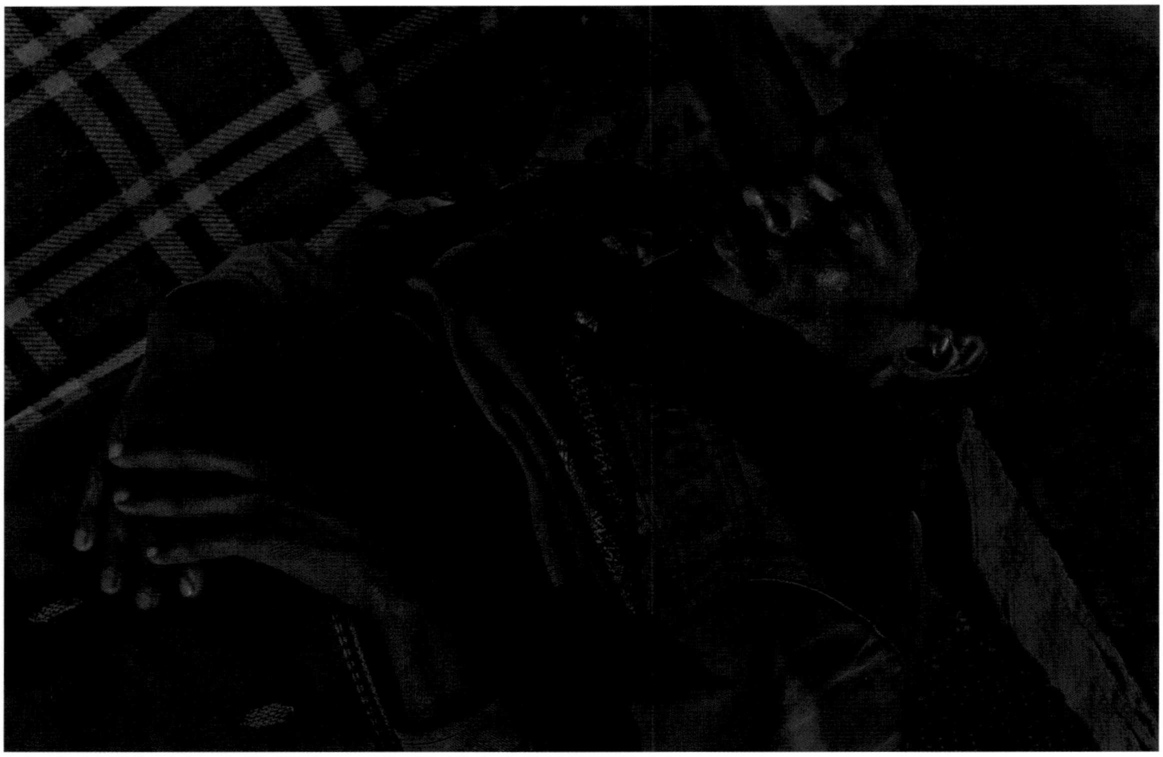

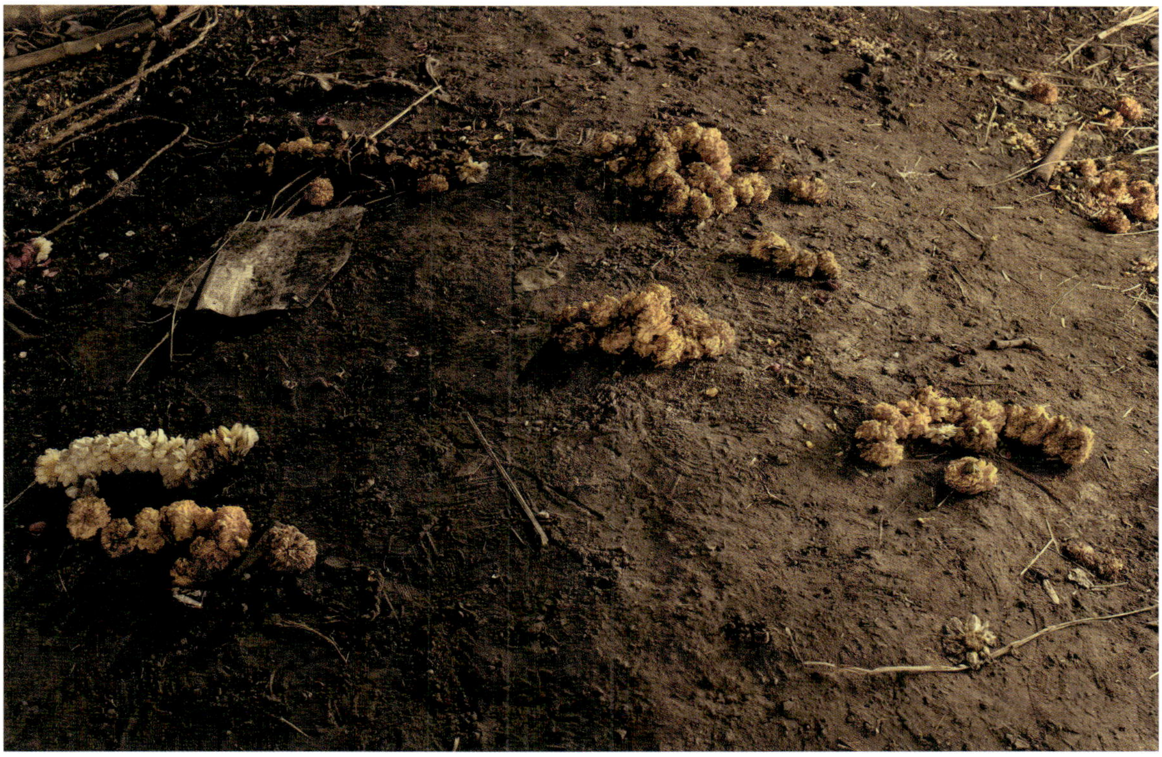

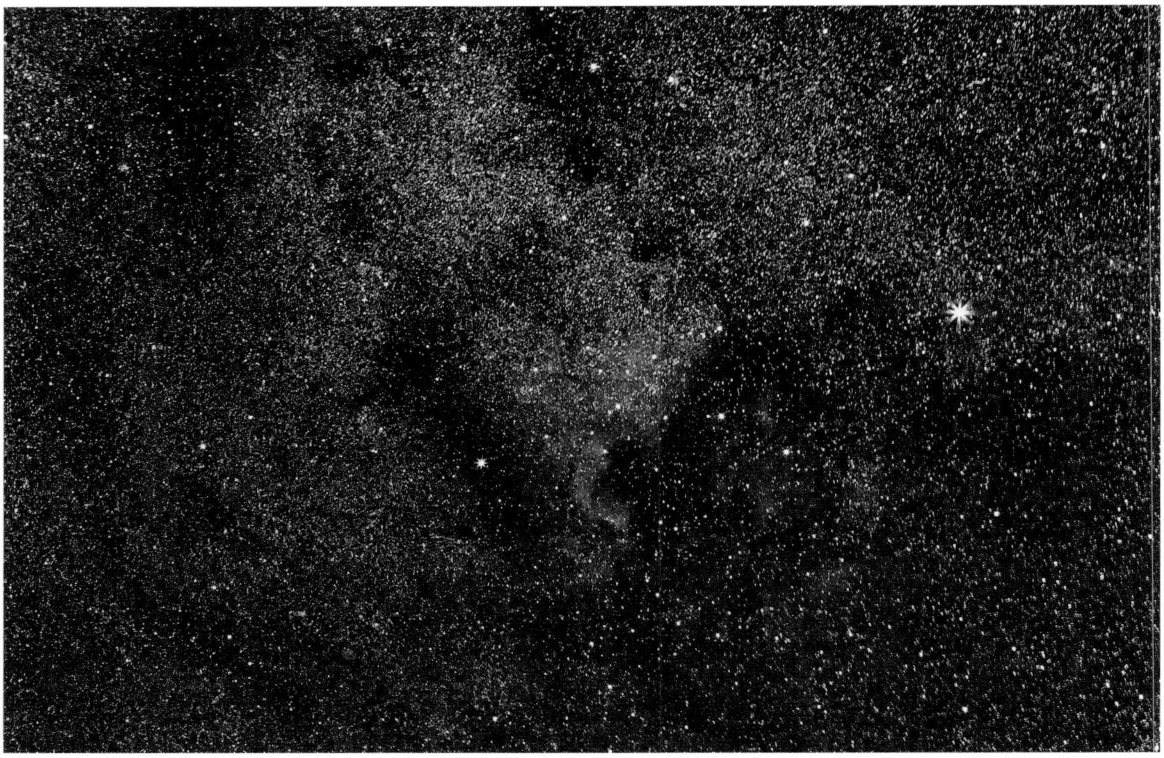

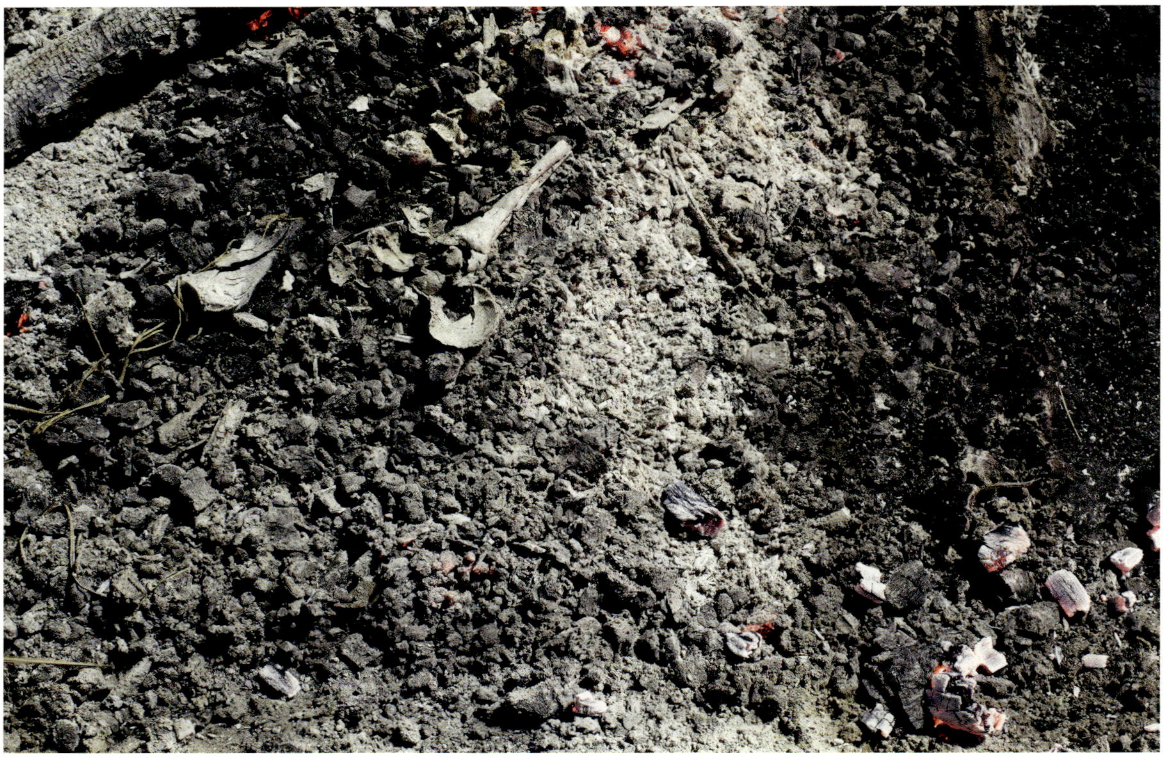

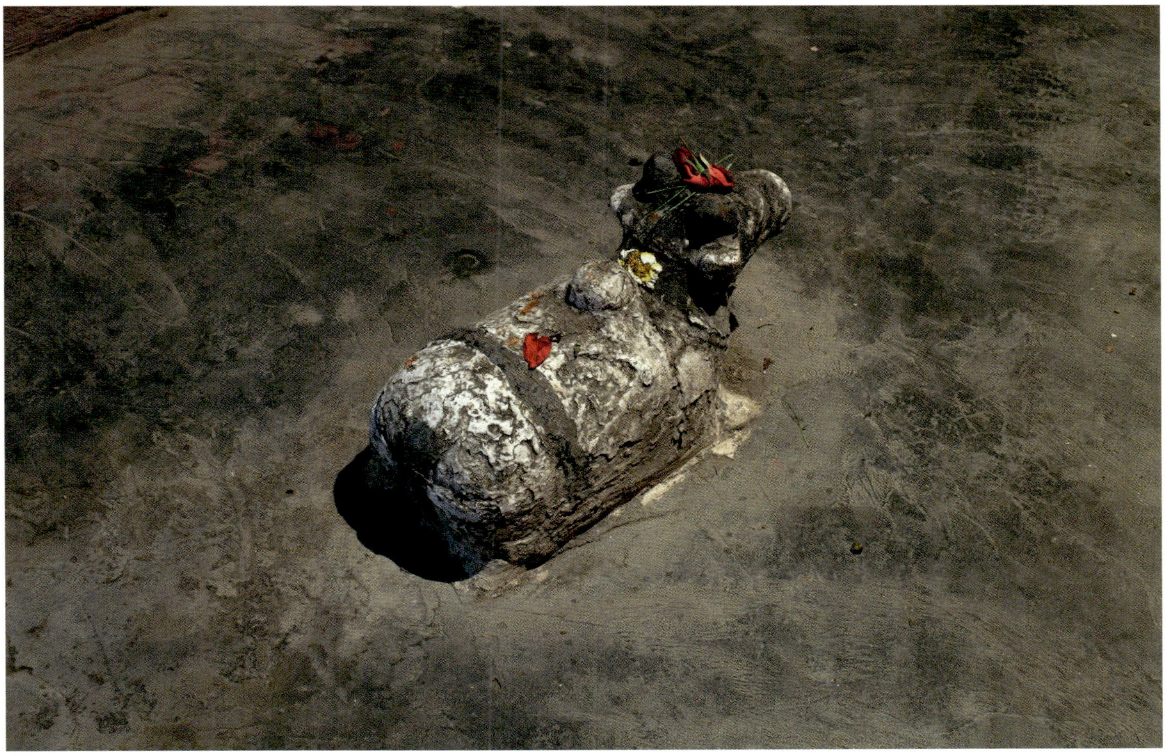

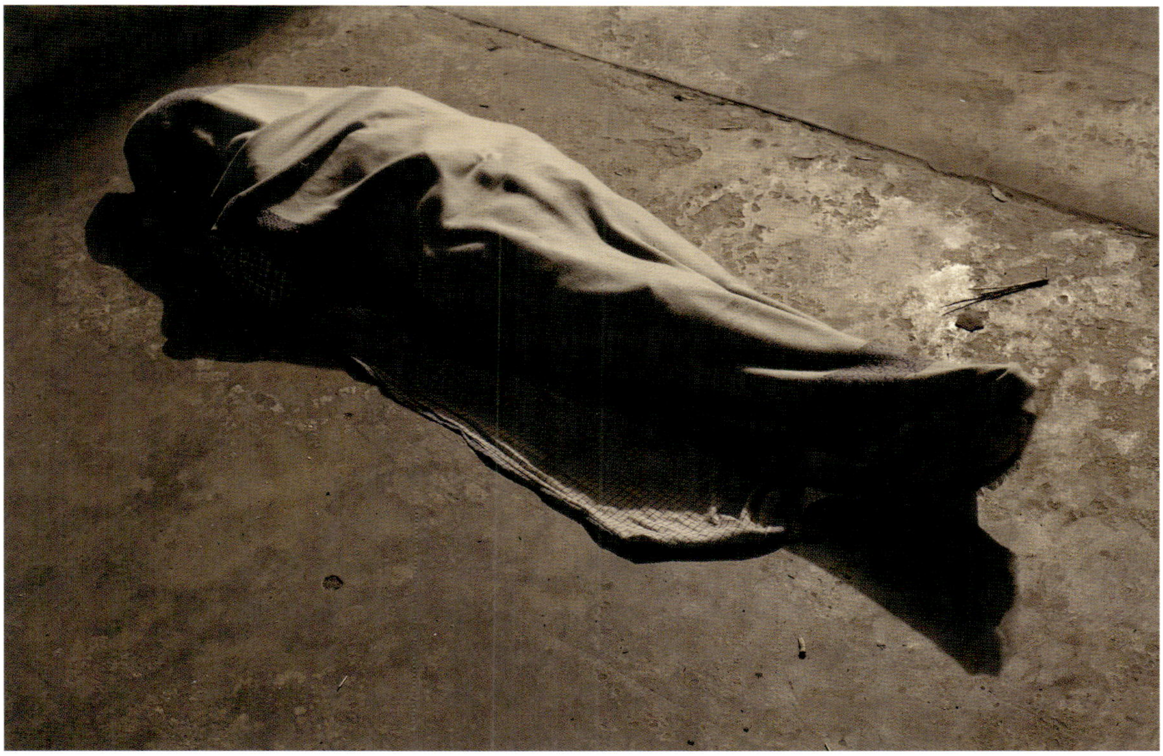

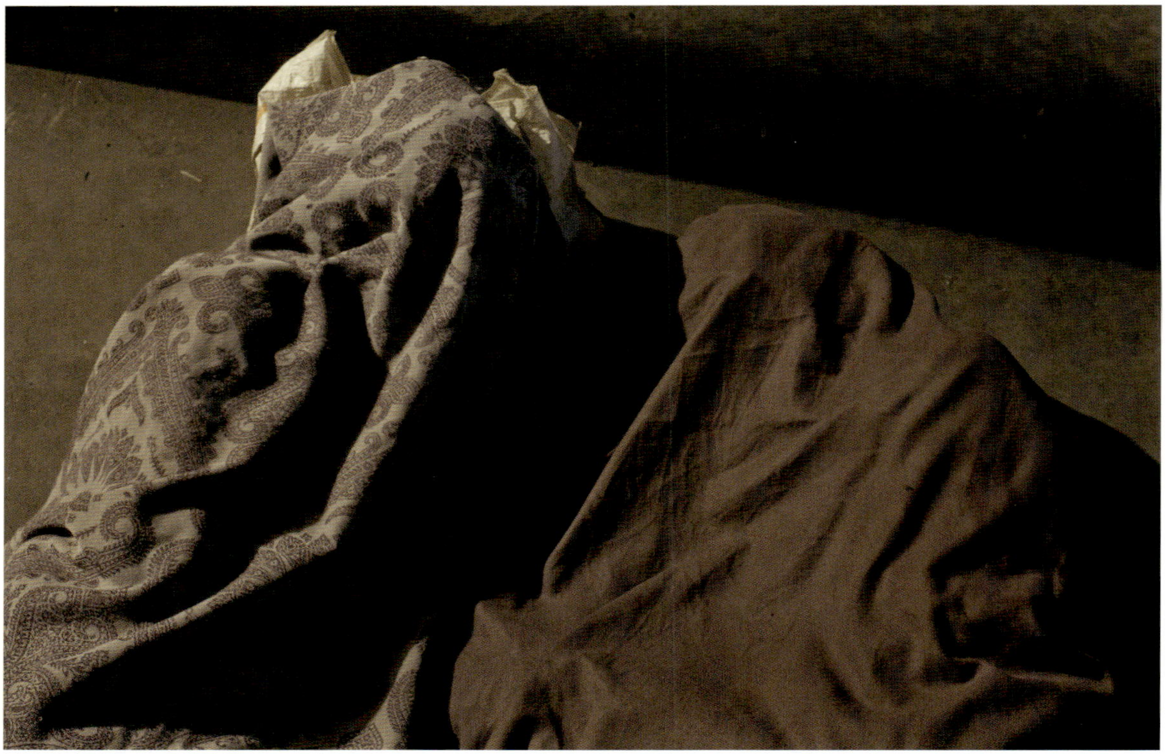

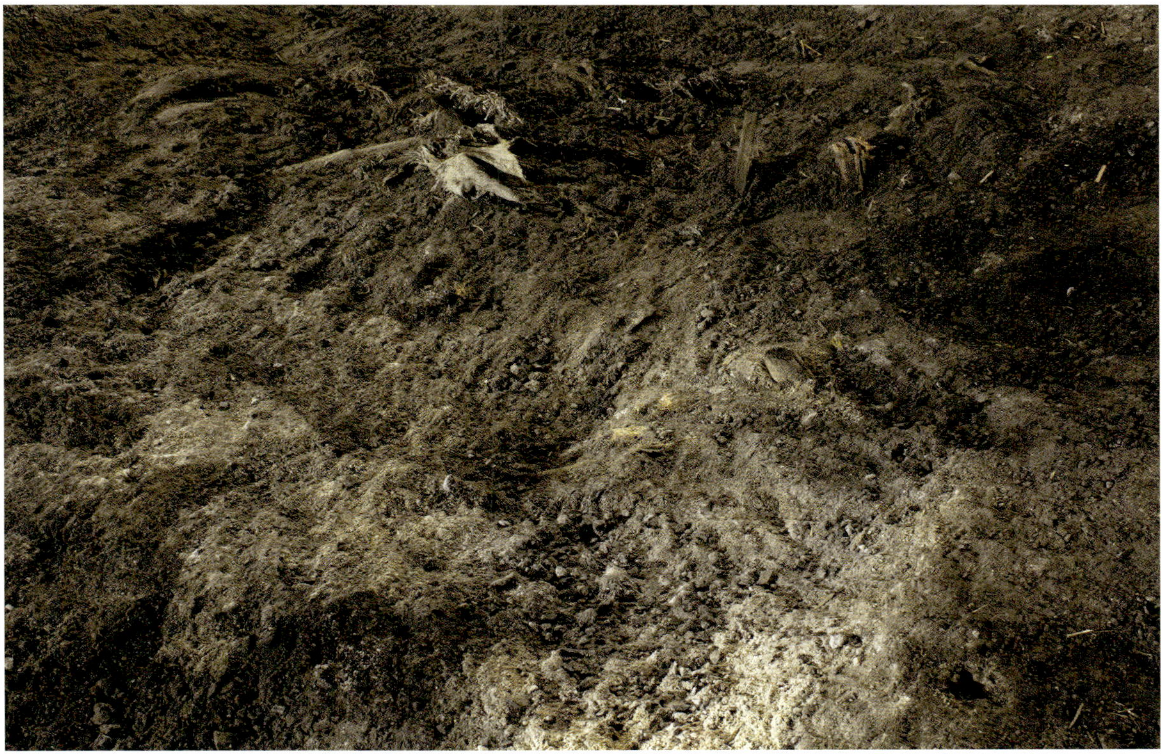

✷

Fazal Sheikh would like to thank the following people for their commitment to this project and its realization: Liz Jobey, Kim Jones, Judith Lange, Peter MacGill, Michael Mack, Petra Manefeld, Ajay Pandey, Nandita Raman, Navneet Raman, Dayanita Singh, Rajkumar Singh, Rakesh Singh

✷

✷

Ether was first exhibited at the Pace/MacGill Gallery, New York
September 7 – October 20 2012

✷

Major support for this publication has been generously provided by the
George Foundation, Winterthur, Switzerland

Support for Fazal Sheikh's projects has been provided
since 2005 by the John D. and Catherine T. MacArthur Foundation

Additional funding provided by the John Simon Guggenheim Memorial Foundation

For more information about Fazal Sheikh's work visit
www.fazalsheikh.org

✷

First edition published in 2013

Book design: Fazal Sheikh, Gerhard Steidl, Bernard Fischer
Text editor: Liz Jobey
Separations: Steidl's digital darkroom
Production and printing: Steidl, Göttingen

Steidl
Düstere Strasse 4 / 37073 Göttingen / Germany
Phone +49 551 49 60 60 / Fax +49 551 49 60 649
mail@steidl.de
www.steidlville.com / www.steidl.de

ISBN 978-3-86930-653-7
Printed in Germany by Steidl